HAROLD CAMERON.

UNITED WE SHALL NOT BE MOVED

UNITED WE SHALL NOT BE MOVED

LOU MACARI

SOUVENIR PRESS

First published 1976 by Souvenir Press Ltd,
43 Great Russell Street, London WC1B 3PA

and simultaneously in Canada by

Methuen Publications,
Agincourt, Ontario

ISBN 0 285 62260 9

Printed in Great Britain by
Bristol Typesetting Co. Ltd,
Barton Manor, St Philips, Bristol

Contents

The author would like warmly to thank Stan Liversedge for his help and advice in compiling this book.

Foreword
by Manchester United Manager, TOMMY DOCHERTY

I never had the slightest hesitation in paying a big transfer fee for Lou Macari; I knew that Manchester United would be getting value for money, when I signed him from Glasgow Celtic. I knew – because I had seen him playing in Scotland and for Scotland . . . in fact, I was the man who introduced little Lou to the international scene.

I was the team manager of Scotland, and I had had my eyes on Lou for quite a while. But he suffered an injury while playing for Celtic, and ligament trouble put him out of action – something he DOESN'T like! – for around six weeks. When I telephoned Jock Stein, the Celtic manager, and told him that I had ideas about giving Lou a run in the international side, he took me up on it straight away. 'You can do yourself – and Lou and Celtic – a favour,' said the big fellow, 'by giving him the chance to regain match fitness.' So I named Lou Macari as one of my Scotland Under-23 players who were taking on the Scotland youth side at Firhill. Lou hadn't played for six weeks; it was a chance for him to ease himself back into the action – and for me to get to know him at close quarters. I saw quite a bit more of him after I had moved to Largs – his home wasn't far away – and I watched him plenty of times when he was playing for his club. So Lou graduated to the ranks of the international squad, and on the occasions when I called the players up for a get-together, he was always included.

By the time I had left my job as Scotland team manager to take charge of Manchester United, Lou was an established first-teamer with Glasgow Celtic and a full-blooded international. And he most definitely was my kind of player. Yet I didn't realise he was available, until I learned that Liverpool had been given permission to talk to him about a transfer to the Merseyside club. And when that didn't materialise, I didn't let the grass grow under my feet: I wanted him for Manchester United.

At the time – it was early in 1973, and only a couple of months after I had gone to Old Trafford myself – I rated Lou a player for the future, with Manchester United. Naturally, I wanted him to go straight into the first team, because I felt even then that he had outstanding ability, but I still believed that his best days were to come. Time has since proved me right – although I have to admit that I was wrong about one thing and, as Lou says frankly in his book, we also have had our differences of opinon.

Looking back, I can see that it has all been good for both of us, and I have no hesitation now in labelling Lou Macari a great footballer, fit to rank alongside others who are world-class players. I mentioned that Lou had some frank things to say in this book, and one chapter deals specifically with yours truly.

Not to be outdone, I've decided that if Lou Macari can write about me, then I can have my say about him. Which is why you will find another contribution from Tommy Docherty further on in the book. I'm delighted here to be able to pay a tribute to someone whom I rate as a great little guy; and it gives me a bit of a kick, too, to tell you a few stories about Lou Macari and present the Tommy Docherty viewpoint on him elsewhere.

So carry on from here, and enjoy reading the story of Lou Macari, not to mention Manchester United. And when you get to the part where Tommy Docherty takes over for a brief spell, I hope you enjoy reading that, too. Lou, I might add, is a great practical joker, and I think it will appeal to his sense of humour when he finds that I've slipped in a wee chapter of my own!

1 This is MY way
by LOU MACARI

This is Lou Macari talking . . . and reminding you that fifty thousand people or more flock to Old Trafford, when Manchester United are playing at home. For the supporters, Old Trafford is their Mecca; and they are ready to cheer the United players on and will them to achieve victory. As the fans jostle each other while crossing the railway bridge and then spread out when they reach the impressive forecourt of the famous ground, they discuss games gone by and look forward to the ninety minutes of action which is to come. Some of those supporters gather outside the official entrance to the ground, and spend a few minutes there, hoping to get a word with or a glimpse of the players who are their heroes. I know: I've seen those supporters gathered outside.

Often, I go to the entrance to meet one or two of my close friends there, and have a brief chat with them before returning inside and going through a ground floor door down the corridor to the United dressing-room. My team-mates will tell you that I'm usually the last man in, about twenty minutes before kick-off time. I'm one of those people who cannot sit still; I have to be occupied doing something. So I don't go into the dressing-room until it's time to get changed into the famous colours which, in years gone by, first earned Manchester United the name of the Red Devils.

Manchester United became world-famous during the late 1950s, when they were crusading in Europe and conquering at home. I was not a part of that scene, of course, but I know that what happened in those days has had a tremendous bearing on the present, and will have on the future.

For under Sir Matt Busby – then United's manager, and before he was honoured with a title – the players forged a reputation which made the name of Manchester United pre-eminent in football. And the reputation has stuck. Today, the name of United is hailed as proudly as ever by their supporters, even though the faces of the playing personnel have changed, and changed again.

On the night that United's manager ended his twenty-five year reign, the team of those days was helping him to sign off with a flourish, by beating derby-game rivals Manchester City 4-3 . . . and Lou Macari was celebrating a grand slam of reserve-team honours with Glasgow Celtic at Brockville, the home of Falkirk. Celtic, dubbed Jock Stein's Babes, added the Second Eleven Cup to the Reserve championship and the League Cup by beating Falkirk reserves 6-1 on aggregate, in front of 2,300 fans. And my thoughts were a long way from Old Trafford.

At that moment in time, I never even dreamed that one day I would be lining up for Manchester United in their famous stadium. My life was centred around the top club in Scotland, Glasgow Celtic, and my dreams were all of winning honours with the club which, in 1967, had become the first from Britain to carry off the European Cup.

Nowadays, I know what it's like to play in front of the roaring thousands who support Manchester United. As I said earlier, they flock to the ground, watch the game and give us their cheers, then depart for home after the ninety minutes of action have ended. Maybe some of them have managed to get an autograph or two.

But few of the 50,000 or so people who have seen the game get to know the players really well. To most of the fans, the Soccer stars are familiar names, people whose faces and playing styles have become familiar, as well. And when you read a book such as this, if you are one of those football fans, you must wonder: 'What's the guy really like?' So I shall try to tell you . . . about myself, and about the people who are my team-mates, and who have become household names in football.

I never object to being asked a straight question – so long as the person doing the asking doesn't object to being given an equally straight answer. So you know just where you stand, from this moment. Apart from football, I have a great love for horse racing, and I am a boxing fan. I cannot say I ever had ambitions to become a jockey, even though at five feet five inches tall I might have stood a chance of making it to the top; but racing fascinates me to the extent that I've always fancied owning a horse which turned out to be a winner – and maybe boxing holds an attraction for me because I regard myself as a fighter, in a different arena. Boxing is an individual sport; Soccer is a team game. But the object of the exercise, in each case, is to make sure of the end product and, so far as I'm concerned, that's very simple. It's all about winning . . . and I have always wanted to be a winner.

I am a professional, in a very professional business, and to me, there are no half-measures about it. Success is the target – it's there to be won. And when anyone asks me about the money side of Soccer, I give them this answer: if you are with a team which is collecting the silverware, you will wind up with medals for yourself. And where there are medals, there is bound to be money.

I don't think it's a matter of being purely mercenary, then. It is a matter of being competitive, sometimes almost fiercely so, and of being eager to take up the sort of challenge which a game such as professional Soccer constantly throws out to you. I used the word 'game', but professional football is much more than that, to the people who are in it. You can believe me when I say that the competitive, combative spirit runs very deeply in me. It's instinctive, and cannot be erased.

I could never go on the field with that half-hearted attitude which suggests that it doesn't really matter, if the opposition does score more goals than your team. When I finish up on the winning side, I'm elated; when I'm on the losing end, I don't feel very pleased, even though I appreciate that there have to be losers, and that you have to learn to accept a defeat, and to try to accept it with dignity. Such as when Manchester United lost the 1976 F.A. Cup final against Southampton. And that, I can assure you, is still a painful memory for me.

No one can be a winner all the time, and my experience over ten years has provided me with ample proof of this, for while I have plenty of medals to show for my endeavours, I also have some bitter memories of days that went sadly wrong. Even with Glasgow Celtic, where I won three Scottish League-championship medals, two Scottish Cup medals and a League Cup medal, I had to accept that there were times when an all-conquering side could come unstuck – and I have a couple of runners-up medals to prove it.

Five years or so ago, Celtic were the red-hot favourites to carry off the League Cup in Scotland . . . but at the end of ninety minutes, they had scored only once and conceded four goals to the under-dogs, Partick Thistle. And found themselves wondering where it had all gone wrong.

I was in the Celtic side that day, and perhaps, when Manchester United went to Wembley to take on Second Division Southampton, the memory of that League Cup-final defeat was revived sufficiently to make me extremely wary of being over-optimistic about United's success. Everyone was making United the raging favourites – the hottest since Wolves, who fell to Portsmouth in the 1939 final – but, from the moment I knew we would be meeting the Saints, I felt that Manchester United must be on a hiding to nothing.

I am not trying to make excuses after the event, or seeking to put a sob-story across to you; if you can recall what I was saying BEFORE the Wembley final was played, you will recognise that, like manager Tommy Docherty and my team-mates, I was playing it very, very cagey. Call it a premonition, but I simply didn't feel happy about the way people were suggesting that Southampton hardly need bother to turn up on the day. Close friends will tell you that I admitted my fears to them . . . and, sadly, events proved me right.

I certainly did not believe that Manchester United were not capable of beating Southampton and carrying off the FA Cup. For the best part of a season, we had shown everyone that we could play exciting, devastating football, and keep up the pace with the clubs who were leading in the race for the League championship. And the way that we brought about the defeat of Derby County in the FA Cup semi-final at Hillsborough was little short of magic, in my opinion. I'm not blowing my own trumpet when I make that claim, either, for I didn't even take part in that match, because of injury.

But all in a couple of weeks or so, there were signs that we might well be running out of luck, just at the stage when we – and any other club challenging for honours – needed it most.

Many a time – at Molineux, for instance, when United won a Cup replay 3-2, after having gone behind – we have swung a game our way. That night against the Wolves, Manchester United showed beyond a shadow of doubt that there was no way they were going to surrender, and go out of the Cup. As I say, that was one instance where we made our own luck, but as the finale of the 1975-76 season approached, I sensed that our luck, and our ability to make things go our way, could just be coming to a full stop.

I shall have more to say about the battle for the First Division championship, and our FA Cup final against Southampton, later in this book. As of now, I'll just add a few more random thoughts so that you get the picture of the kind of professional footballer I consider myself to be.

I was mad about playing football almost from the moment I could walk, so there must be something in what people say about individuals having a particular gift for a particular job. As I began to grow into my teens, Celtic were the ones I idolised. Yet there came a day when, in spite of – or more probably, because of – having won so much as a player at Parkhead, I wanted to make the break, pack my bags and head for England.

It was ambition that was driving me on; ambition and the feeling that there was a new challenge for me. I had to wait quite a while, but the day did dawn when Celtic said offici-ally that they were prepared to let me go, if some other club were prepared to pay them £200,000 for the privilege of signing me. That club, in the first instance, turned out to be Liverpool, and one day in January 1973 I travelled south to talk to their manager, Bill Shankly. Little more than twenty-four hours later, I was back in Scotland . . . and signing the forms which made me a Manchester United player.

A lot of people, I imagine, couldn't weigh up why I had turned my back on the chance to sign for the Anfield club, and so quickly made the move to Old Trafford, which was only thirty miles or so down the East Lancashire road from Liverpool. For Liverpool, clearly, were heading for success – yet again – and Manchester United, equally obviously, seemed to be heading for the Second Division. But I had my own reasons for making what a lot of folk thought was an astonishing decision, and I was ready enough to take my chance of swimming or sinking with Tommy Docherty's team.

I wouldn't be honest if I didn't admit that after I had joined United, there were times when I began to wonder if I had made the most ghastly mistake of my footballing life; and even now, with several years to go before I have to hang up my playing boots, I know that there will be other occasions when I shall question the way that my career has gone, and the decisions I have made.

I shall certainly have questions to ask myself, for instance, if I wind up without a League-championship or FA Cup-winner's medal, after my time spent at Old Trafford . . . because, let me remind you, I said at the start that I want nothing more than to be hailed as a winner. In the hours after Manchester United's FA Cup-final defeat against Southampton, I pondered the future, thought more than once about Liverpool, and reflected wryly on the might-have-beens.

For while United faltered and faded from the race for the League championship, and lost the FA Cup, Liverpool went on to win not only the title, but the UEFA Cup, as they had done three years earlier – in the very season, you will recall, I first settled for Manchester United. Had I gone to Anfield, in the space of three years I would have collected five medals – always assuming of course that I had been able to claim a first-team place!

Yes, I believe that I would have held down a first-team spot at Anfield. Apart from anything else, I'll give Bill Shankly the credit for making sure he went for genuine talent, when he tried to sign a player. And today, somewhere deep inside me there remains that burning force which people call ambition. It's what led me to leave Glasgow Celtic in the first place and – who knows? – it's what might one day take me back across the Border. For although I have often said I fancied running a bookmaker's business when I have to call it a day as a player, I know instinctively that I shall not want to turn my back upon the game.

And I have a dream . . . of going home, maybe to manage Celtic, the club which first showed me what being a winner was all about. Chance, they say, is a fine thing – and I may never get the chance to return to Parkhead, save as a spectator. But if you don't dream dreams, you stagnate. And I never was one who could settle happily for mediocrity. Plenty of people have called me many things in my time as a professional footballer, and not all the descriptions of me have been complimentary. But I know myself well enough to be sure that I can give as well as I can take, that I can accept the knocks and come back fighting. I am the sort of character who becomes all the more determined to prove detractors wrong, and I believe I have done this to good effect since I arrived at Manchester United. For it wasn't all easy going, during my first year or so there.

I also like to do things my way – the way I feel is right for me. Once or twice, I have to admit, my way has turned out to be the wrong way, and I have ended up having to accept my punishment. That, however, has helped me to mature, while not lessening my determination to succeed.

Everybody likes to be liked, yet I know that you cannot be popular with everybody all the time. Managers and players are heroes, when they are winning things; when they are struggling for success, the gloss can disappear almost overnight. Yet you can only do your best, the way you see it, and that, I think, is what I have done in my career so far. One day, perhaps, I shall feel that I know all the answers, when I look back upon my career in football; but the end of my career as a player, I hope, is a long time distant yet. And meanwhile, I shall continue striving to be a winner.

2 Success with Celtic

There were only two teams in Scotland, so far as the folk
in and around Glasgow – and even further afield – were concerned. One was Rangers . . . and they were not the team
for me. The other was Celtic . . . and my boyhood dream
was to play for them. When I achieved that ambition, I
came to realise that in their manager, Jock Stein, I had met
a wise man. He knew his Soccer, as other craftsmen know
their trade; and he had long ago realised, and come to accept, that players were not all cast in the same mould. And
because he recognised that I had to play the game my way,
he let me get on with it. So Lou Macari prospered, along
with Glasgow Celtic.

Most people know that my family has an Italian background on my father's side, although the strain goes a long
way back, because both my father and mother could claim
to be pure Scottish. However, while I speak with a genuine
Scots accent, too, few people probably realise that I spent
the early years of my life down in the south of England.

My father, who is dead now, owned a cafe in London and,
like so many Scots, he had a passion for football. The
amateurs of Leytonstone were his team; in fact, he played
for them. And I became their mascot. I was two years old,
and dressed to suit the part in football boots, socks, and a
red-and-white strip with the number 10 on the back of the
jersey. And when Leytonstone went out to play the opposition, I went out with them.

Maybe my instinct for the game, and the competitive
side of my nature, were strongly in evidence even so early

in my life, for my first appearance as a mascot ended with the Macari bairn being carried off the field, tearful and howling. I wanted to stay and enjoy the fun, be a part of it all and get into the action. I grew to learn of course that little boys could not compete against the men, but my passion for the game deepened with every year that passed. Yes, even though the school that I attended in those days did not cater for a game as rough as football.

I had been born in Edinburgh, but the family moved to London when I was only six months old, and I remained in the south of England until I was going on for ten. It was then, when we moved back north of the Border, that I got my first real chance to show that I had a talent for playing football; for once we had settled down at our house in Kilwinning, which is on the coast between Glasgow and Largs, I was sent to a school where Soccer was not only recognised as a sport fit to play – it was actively encouraged as the right kind of therapy for lads with energy to spare.

Most youngsters play football at school, of course, but my school, St Michael's, near Largs, produced a team which I can modestly claim was exceptional. Maybe our ambitions were fostered, too, by the fact that the Scotland international side used Largs as their training headquarters.

In any event, St Michael's won just about every trophy for which they competed, in my day, and so I became accustomed to being a winner, even then. I said the team was exceptional, and this is borne out by the fact that no fewer than seven of the members of that schoolboy side went on to join professional clubs in Scotland, although I should add that not everyone scaled the heights.

By the time I arrived at Parkhead, I had gained my first representative honours in football, for I had been selected as a Scotland schoolboy international, and I fervently hoped that it was only a foretaste of many more honours at an even higher level. My strong suit was that I could score goals. It was this ability which had prompted one of the top clubs from England to keep a close eye on me, and had I been of a mind to do so I could easily have returned across the Border and tried my luck with Wolves. That Wolves scout seemed to be on the touchline every time I played – and he wasn't the only one taking an interest in me.

Morton had ideas about my joining them, but – and I say this without any disrespect – they were regarded as small fish in the Scottish Soccer sea, and my single-minded ambition was to show Celtic that I was a player they just had to take. I was just turned fourteen when Celtic made their interest known by inviting me to go training at Parkhead a couple of nights a week.

That meant a fifteen mile train journey to Glasgow, and it also meant that I was tired out by the time I returned home. But my parents were ready to offer me every encouragement – not that it was needed – and my ambitions were spurred even more when Celtic eventually offered me the chance to sign for them as an apprentice professional.

Before I joined them as a player, I had been one of their most avid supporters, and I travelled hundreds of miles to see them play. The thrill of following them and cheering them to victory paled into insignificance, however, once they had asked me to join them. Being 'in' was the greatest thing that had happened to me and, at the time, it seemed the summit of my footballing ambitions. Probably, then, the thought did not cross my mind that I would ever want to leave; but time brings many changes.

Celtic had opened the doors of Parkhead to me shortly after I had made two appearances for Scotland schoolboys, against England and Wales, so I was on the way to becoming – I hoped – a first-team player with Scotland's premier club (indeed, Scotland's ONLY club, so far as I was concerned). And I think it's worth making a point here about schoolboy Soccer generally, and my own ideas in particular.

I didn't bother unduly about the position in which I played – it was sufficient that I regarded myself as a forward who liked to be in the thick of the action. I had sufficient energy to cover every blade of grass on the park, and I didn't feel I had done my job until I had left my footmarks just about everywhere. However, my father clearly had spotted that I had the knack of being on the right spot at the right time for scoring goals, and he took some pains to hammer it into my head that goals were the end-product everyone wanted.

So I followed his advice, and consciously went out with the idea that to make my mark, I had to get my name on the scoresheet. I must admit, too, that tucking the ball away gave me a considerable kick; and when I did arrive at Parkhead I had every reason to be grateful to the backroom staff there for not drilling tactics into me and stifling my natural skills and sheer appetite for the game.

Today, youngsters often seem to be too much aware of team formations even before they have begun to learn to kick a football properly. And the cult of playing the game by numbers and positions can be too rigidly imposed, so that kids forget – or don't even realise – they have a natural aptitude for doing something especially well. At one time, not so long ago, the term 'midfield player' became so fashionable that almost every lad who was asked what position he played would produce those two words as his answer.

Maybe it's my inherent Scottish pride (some might call it prejudice), but despite my later ambitions to see if I measured up to the demands of top-class football in England, I still feel that north of the Border they produce players who have more flair when it comes to doing what is natural – which means playing what you might call 'pure' football. Scottish skills are something of which we can be proud, and English football has plenty of reason to be grateful to many of the men who have made the trek south.

I don't really care if a lad comes from north or south of the Border, or even from Timbuktoo: if he has a natural skill, it should not be stifled by tactics and team strategies.

In many ways, Denis Law was a law unto himself, yet he proved to the world that he had a natural, priceless aptitude for tucking away the scoring chances. Other footballers have an instinctive ability to pinpoint a forty-yard pass, or to take on a man and leave him flat-footed. And I feel it is important that any youngster who shows he possesses an exceptional skill in a particular department of the game should be encouraged to utilise it to the full.

I must always be grateful to Celtic and Jock Stein that they didn't stuff my head with ideas about the sort of game THEY were determined I should play. What had attracted Celtic to me, in the first instance, was the fact that I was a busy little footballer who, in addition, seemed to have the flair for nipping into the eighteen-yard box at the right moment and putting the ball into the back of the net. In Jock Stein I had a manager who, when I did break through to first-team football, simply gave me the right to go out, enjoy my game as I had always played it – and score goals. 'The nearest thing to Jimmy Greaves' was one description of me, and that's flattering, I know, because Greaves was a goal-poacher supreme. But I never aspired to be Greaves the second; my idea was to make my reputation in the way I knew best, and scoring goals was the job I enjoyed doing. It still is, too.

After that little piece of self-advertising, perhaps I had better try to justify my talk about being a marksman, so I'll mention that when I broke through to Celtic's first team, I did the job they asked, by sticking the ball into the net fourteen times during the first couple of months or so of the season. And I have scored my share of goals since I arrived in English football.

My goals for Celtic included a hat-trick against Airdrie, and in season 1971-72 I collected my first Scotland Under-23 cap. By the time the parting of the ways came at Parkhead, I had winner's medals in the League, the Scottish Cup and the League Cup, so I can look back on some stirring

days in Scottish football. And as usual Celtic were competing in Europe, season by season, so I got a taste of what it is
like to come up against some of the crack Continental
sides.

I had been thrilled when, in 1967, Celtic won the European Cup-final duel against Inter-Milan, although I was then
only on the fringe of professional football; once I got into
the first team, my instinct for top-class competition was
plainly in evidence again, as I welcomed the chance to show
that I could meet and match world-class players.

One of the lasting memories of my days at Parkhead
concerns the time Celtic came up against the Hungarians
of Ujpest Dosza, in the quarter-finals of the European Cup,
some six years after I had moved up from schoolboy football. The first leg of the tie was played in Budapest, and
Celtic were doing nicely, with the score 1–1, and the final
five minutes beginning to tick away. Celtic got possession
and went forward, as they have always done when given the
opportunity to attack, and Kenny Dalglish hit a shot which
rebounded to me. I was in the right spot, and my goal-
poaching instinct served me well, as I slotted the ball home.

There was an interesting sidelight to my winner in
Budapest, for one of Celtic's greatest supporters was a
Glasgow bookmaker called Tony Queen, who followed the
team around Europe, as well as at home. He saw that
quarter-final tie in Hungary, and leaped for joy when I
scored that goal. But he had somewhat mixed feelings, when
the realisation dawned that it had cost him no less than
£10,000! In fact, he admitted that when it sank home, he
would have been happier had we drawn – and I can't say I
blame him for that sentiment.

How come my goal was so expensive for him? He had
offered odds of 4-1 against Celts defeating Ujpest Dosza
on their own territory, and so much cash poured in that
the odds were then reduced to 3-1. When he arrived back
in Glasgow after the match, and went to his office, he dis-

covered that the goal I had scored had made a difference of £10,000 to his business. Still, that's life.

The game itself lives on in my mind, for although we won 2-1, I was the only Celtic player to get his name on the scoresheet. It was a nightmare start for the Hungarian side, because they were a goal down in the first fifteen minutes. When we attacked, Jim Brogan crossed the ball – and Ujpest defender Josef Horvath headed it past his own goalkeeper. At half-time that was still the only goal between us, then Horvath got his own back, for he rammed in an equaliser from all of thirty yards. It was a thundering piledriver of a shot which gave our 'keeper, Evan Williams, not the ghost of a chance.

Evan made a string of fine saves after that, the Hungarians claimed twice for penalties – they must have been joking! – and with only four minutes remaining, I knocked in the winner.

The Glasgow bookie may have had some private reservations about it all, but Celtic manager Jock Stein was in an expansive mood, as he said: 'At this level, and when you consider the age of this team of ours, it is probably Celtic's best European Cup display since Lisbon' (when the Parkhead club had won the trophy against Inter-Milan, in 1967).

The critics happily conceded that there had not been one single failure in the Celtic side – 'not only at times did they run Ujpest into the ground . . . they played with an elegant skill which brought admiration from the partisan home fans.'

I was described as 'a ninety-minute terrier for Celtic' who 'capped a magnificent show with a typical goal, showing all the coolness of a European veteran to make a chance for himself in a crowded goal area.'

Celtic had played a storming game, and commanded the middle of the park, where we had Bobby Murdoch (who later went to Middlesbrough), David Hay (signed later by Chelsea), Kenny Dalglish and Harry Hood operating and in top form. And figuring at right-back was a youngster who has proved to be a thorn in the side of England, as well as of European opponents, in recent seasons – Danny McGrain, whom many people now regard as the best attacking defender in Britain.

As for the Hungarian supporters, they were sporting enough to applaud our victory, but those 30,000 fans certainly had glum looks on their faces as they filed sorrowfully from the stadium. They sensed that their team had lost the chance of going through to the semi-finals of the European Cup. And they were right – but Ujpest still had to be beaten.

Celtic don't usually give the opposition much chance when they are playing at Parkhead, but it was Ujpest Dosza who handed out a shock for the Scottish fans when they scored a goal in the first five minutes of that second-leg match, and so we had it all to do again. There was less than half an hour of the game to go when I got the chance for the second time in that tie to swing the match Celtic's way, and my goal at Parkhead was the killer. Celtic went through to their third European Cup semi-final in six years, and the cheers from the 75,000 people packing the ground were like music in my ears.

I have never claimed to be the world's most complete footballer, although I have always believed I had my fair share of skills, but I can say without fear of contradiction that I usually thrive on big occasions, and while I get that keyed-up feeling before a game, once I'm in the thick of the action, I am not plagued by nerves. On the contrary, I feel the adrenalin flowing, and I'm ready to take my chances when I get into the target area to snap up scoring opportunities. I believe that to get goals, you've got to be prepared to go where it can hurt, as well as being sharp enough to spot the openings and poach the goals.

Temperamentally, I'm suited to the big-time atmosphere, the roaring crowds and the sense of being involved in a great occasion. In the 1971 Scottish Cup final, I was on the mark to help Celtic score a 2-1 replay win over their great rivals, Rangers, and the following season, when Celtic thrashed Hibs 6-1, I collected a couple of the goals which kept the Cup at Parkhead.

After having helped Celtic to secure a place in the semi-finals of the European Cup, I was on my mettle when we clashed with Hearts at Tynecastle the following Saturday in the quarter-finals of the Scottish Cup, and again I scored a goal which clinched a semi-final place for the Parkhead club. Kilmarnock barred our way to Hampden, and once more I hit the target as we applied the knock-out blow to Killie; then, as I have just mentioned, we waltzed round Hibs by scoring a 6-1 victory in the final.

As they had done in 1967, Celtic took on Inter-Milan in the European Cup, but this time instead of playing in Lisbon, we had to travel to the famous San Siro stadium in Milan for the first leg of the tie. If you've never experienced a European match there, you have missed something, even as a spectator. The Italian fans are every bit as fervent as the most rabid Glaswegians, and they don't hesitate to let you know what they think of your chances, as the team coach runs the gauntlet and the driver tries to steer a way through the throng milling around the stadium. Those fans indicate in no uncertain manner that they reckon you'll be given a hiding.

Italian football has long been noted, too, for the fact that defences so often dominate, because they have perfected the art of stifling the opposition, and Inter have been among the leading exponents of this technique, as teams such as Liverpool and Everton would confirm. The night Celtic played Inter in the San Siro stadium, though, the boot was on the other foot, because it was Celtic who defied the Italians to find a way through, and when the game ended without a goal having been scored, we were confident that we would be meeting Ajax or Benfica in the final.

But the Italians had the last laugh, for when they played the second leg of the tie at Parkhead, they showed that while they could defend well, they could also break swiftly, and with menace. We were sick with disappointment when Inter just managed to get the better of us, but there was nothing we could do but take it.

I have three scrapbooks of cuttings which single out some of the highlights of my career – and the occasional low point. One scrapbook contains a programme for that semi-final tie at Parkhead against Inter . . . but that's as far as it goes. When it comes to the point, I don't really want any souvenirs of the sad occasions – I told you, remember, that I want to be a winner.

So even now I prefer to think of the good times, rather than dwell upon that sad night at Parkhead. The good times included getting into Scotland's full international squad and going to Brazil for the mini-World Cup tournament which marked the centenary of the Brazilian Football Association. That was when I first felt the real impact of the man who has become known throughout football as The Doc. For Tommy Docherty, who had had his own ups and downs in a managerial career which had taken him to Chelsea, Aston Villa, Rotherham and Oporto, was the team boss of the Scotland international side. The two of us have had our ups and downs, too, as I shall tell you later.

At that stage I never dreamed, though, that one day we would be at the same club . . . Manchester United. But that didn't mean to say I hadn't had my own private dreams of conquering new fields – south of the Border.

And if that last remark seems to indicate a sense of disloyalty to Celtic, I firmly dispute it, here and now. You might wonder how any player could think of leaving a club with which he had tasted so much success. Three Scottish League-championship medals, two Scottish Cup medals, a League Cup medal and two League Cup runners-up medals

. . . those were the very tangible momentoes of what Celtic had done for me, and I would be the last to deny it.

But I have already told you the sort of guy I am, and I make no apology for repeating it now. I thrive on the stimulus of a new challenge, and competing for Celtic against Rangers, season by season – for that, in effect, was what Scottish football was about – had begun to pall. I could only win the same medals again . . . and again . . . and again.

You will have heard and read what happens when players get into an international side, especially if they are from clubs in the lower divisions. Their horizons are widened overnight, and so are their ambitions. And I for one don't blame a player if he feels that he wants to join a club which, like the international team, can give him a taste of the big-time and maybe European competition.

It wasn't quite like that, in my case, for Celtic were THE club in Scotland, bar none; but I felt that I could achieve very little more with them, even if there was the chance of winning something in Europe virtually every season. I'm a restless sort of a guy, too, and I felt that a change could turn out to be as good as a rest.

Frankly, I wanted to find out if the First Division in England was all that it was cracked up to be. I hoped it was – because I also wanted to find out if I could measure up to even more demanding standards, by playing against top-flight opposition every week of the season. Let's face it, how many clubs north of the Border can really claim to be somebody?

Even Rangers, in my days with Celtic, were generally second-best to the Parkhead club, which effectively meant that they were also-rans. Hibs, Hearts and Aberdeen might occasionally produce a shock result, but Celtic were what Scottish football was really all about. And for me, England seemed a new and attractive proposition.

When you've done just about everything in your own

country, so far as football at the top is concerned, and you're still only twenty-two, the prospect of another ten years doing the same thing begins to lose its excitement. Celtic-daft I may have been (and I suppose that I shall always remain a Celt at heart), but I also had itchy feet. One day, maybe, those feet will become itchy again and I shall move back north of the Border to manage. And THAT, if I ever got the chance, would spell out another and different sort of challenge . . . just supposing that Celtic were looking for a new manager at the time!

3 The Parting of The Ways

After five years as a Celtic player, I put in a written application for a transfer. The option clause on my contract was nearing its end, and Celtic and I could not agree about the terms of a new contract, although the club was ready to re-engage me for a six-year spell. After a considerable amount of talking behind closed doors, we still couldn't reach agreement, and finally Celtic said I would be allowed to leave, if and when they received what they termed a 'suitable' offer for me. That was in April 1971.

One month later, Lou Macari and Glasgow Celtic had buried the hatchet. I withdrew my transfer request and signed a new, five-year contract. Three days later, my spell of uncertainty had come to an end, for I was drafted into the side which played Rangers in the final of the Scottish Cup, at Hampden Park – and celebrated by scoring the first goal in Celtic's 2-1 victory, which made it a double for the club, because they had already captured the League championship. More than 100,000 people saw that final – a replay of the previous Saturday's game – and I picked up my first Cup-winner's medal.

I settled down, and looked ahead to a career which had begun and, I felt, would probably end with Celtic, and the honours came thick and fast, over the next couple of years. But by the end of 1972, I was about to part company with Celtic, for good – although I didn't know it, at the time. Once again, I had asked for a move, and the club and I had agreed to keep things quiet until the Christmas and New Year matches were out of the way. But that didn't mean to say I was going to get my way at once, although I was hopeful that there would be swift developments, once Celtic broke the news that I had asked to go.

My sights were on England, and I felt that it was the right time for me to take the plunge. My wife, Dale, was expecting our first baby, and it seemed that it was the moment to begin a new family life elsewhere. Dale is an American, but we had met years earlier, when she attended the same school as myself – her father, an executive with an American company, had worked for a couple of years at Largs, then the family had returned to the US. And I had flown across the Atlantic to be married.

I knew that I owed a great deal to Celtic and to their manager, Jock Stein, who is a very canny fellow. He knew my make-up, and all through my years at Parkhead, he had allowed me to play the kind of game I felt suited me best – which meant giving me a virtually free role, and allowing me to play an attacking game, within the framework of the team pattern. When the parting of the ways had first been mooted, he had told me that Liverpool had been in touch about me – something like a year previously – but I gathered he had then told Bill Shankly there was nothing doing, although if the situation changed, he added, Liverpool, would be the first club to know.

I saw in the New Year of 1973 still as a Celtic player, but before many days had passed, I knew that Celtic were about to sell me. I was called into the office one day, and told that an English First Division club had been inquiring about me, although at that stage, Celtic were not prepared to go any further. So I had to contain my curiosity about the club's identity for a while longer. Naturally, I wondered if the club were Liverpool.

The speculation had been intense, once the news of my impending departure had broken, and immediately the two clubs linked with me were Liverpool and Manchester United. There was speculation that the transfer fee would be a record £200,000, which would top the price Everton had paid to Aberdeen for striker Joe Harper. And Tommy Docherty, who had recently vacated his job as Scotland's team manager, to take charge at Old Trafford, was asked about Manchester United's interest in me. He said there had been too much speculation recently – United had already spent hundreds of thousands of pounds on new recruits – and added : 'I am not saying anything.'

The forecast was that there would be a tug-of-war between United and Liverpool for my services, and reference was made to the fact that Tommy Docherty, as Scotland's manager, had chosen me half a dozen times for international outings, and it was also mentioned that I was the only Celtic player who had agreed to go with The Doc and his Scotland team to Brazil for the mini-World Cup the previous summer. The day Celtic announced that I was for sale, Manchester United had lost 3-1 at Highbury against Arsenal, and were propping up the rest of the First Division clubs. Speculation was heightened, because United had a £200,000 striker, Ted MacDougall, on the substitutes' bench at Highbury. So was it going to be Macari in, and MacDougall out?

I wasn't concerned with anything other than my own future, but I knew I would have to wait and see what happened. Further news was not long delayed, however, because my telephone rang at midnight, and the call revealed the name of the club which had made the move to sign me. It was Liverpool; and I was also told that a car would be round first thing in the morning, to take me to the station. I couldn't see why the call had had to wait until midnight, in the first place, and I didn't get much sleep during the hours of darkness that were left, as I pondered on what was likely to happen the following day.

The car duly arrived, and I caught the train south, arriving in Liverpool in time to watch Bill Shankly's team play Burnley in a third-round FA Cup replay, at Anfield. The date was January 16, and Liverpool won, 3-0. That Tuesday night, they were taking time off from the battle for the League championship, but they were sitting pretty at the top of the First Division, leading Arsenal by three points, after 26 matches. And they were still going strong in the UEFA Cup competition. Manchester United, with 17 points from 25 games, were 23 adrift of the Anfield club, and I reckon that most people must have made them second favourites to sign me . . . if, of course, they came in, as well.

Tommy Docherty was at Anfield that night to see the game, and as he chatted to other visitors to Anfield, in the lounge upstairs, after the match, I was face to face with Bill Shankly, in his office down the corridor on the ground floor. Not surprisingly, Bill Shankly spoke with great enthusiasm of his ambitions for Liverpool, of the players he already had at his disposal . . . and of the part he wanted me to play in the future success of the club. And when Bill Shankly is in full flow, he is a persuasive man.

But somewhere in my make-up, there is a mule-like streak of stubbornness, and I wasn't going to be persuaded so easily. Deep down, I felt that, like it or not, I was being channelled towards the Anfield club. I certainly didn't blame Liverpool one iota for having stepped in with their offer, which was obviously acceptable to Celtic; nor did I blame Bill Shankly for making every effort to convince me that I would serve my own interests best by joining them. But I couldn't get rid of the feeling that Celtic had set things up without my having really been consulted. And that stubborn streak was very much in evidence, as I decided that I wanted time to think about things, before making up my mind.

There were various factors involved, and these included Liverpool's bid for the double of League championship and UEFA Cup. They were clearly such a successful side that I wondered if I could really contribute anything further. It might well turn out to be Celtic all over again, and I wasn't sure I would feel there was sufficient challenge in it to act as a personal spur to me. From what I had heard and read of the situation, also, everyone seemed to have the idea that I was going to replace Welsh international John Toshack in the Liverpool side, and I didn't much like such a ready assumption.

Possibly I misread the situation, or read more into it than was true; but my ultimate assessment of matters was that I wasn't going to be pushed into a quick signing which I might, or might not, regret within a very short space of time. And at that moment, time was something I wanted, to consider all the angles. For I was on the verge of taking the biggest step in my footballing career.

Within 24 hours, there was another factor I had to take into my calculations. Manchester United. They had now made their move, and it seemed they were prepared to match Liverpool so far as the transfer fee was concerned. So I was given the go-ahead to talk to Tommy Docherty . . . who, it was suggested, was on the point of selling Ted MacDougall to West Ham. What happened between Manchester United, West Ham and Ted MacDougall was not really my concern; what happened between Manchester United and Lou Macari was. And I took a long, hard look at United's situation in the First Division . . .

They had been one of the great teams of the 1950s and the 1960s, but their present position was in stark contrast to that of Liverpool. While the Anfield club were lording it at the top, Manchester United, despite a flurry of spending, were candidates for the Second Division. So when I talked to Tommy Docherty, I weighed up my own prospects, as well as United's. If I decided to join them, I would certainly be going in at the deep end – but which club, as he pointed out to me, could offer a greater challenge to a player who claimed he thrived on challenges?

I realised that if I moved to Anfield, I would be going to a club where success was already assured . . . and I'd known nothing but success in my career at Glasgow Celtic. You

B

may suspect that I was a little afraid of signing for Liverpool, in case I didn't measure up to their high standards, and I'll admit that point didn't escape me, either. But the truth is that I have never needed anyone to convince me about my own ability; so I had no feelings of inferiority, or fears of being labelled a failure.

If I joined Manchester United, I would be accepting a great deal of responsibility, considering their perilous situation at the foot of the First Division. Yet I couldn't help but feel that United were such a big club, in every sense of the word, and that I was being offered the chance to be a part of a revival which would bring back the glory days to Old Trafford. Tommy Docherty convinced me that whatever happened that season – and he was determined to keep United in the top flight – there was only one way the club was going to travel, in the future . . . and that was back to the top. Which was where Liverpool already were.

So I took a deep breath, and decided to take the plunge. All in the space of a couple of days, I had had the chance to join two of the top clubs in English League football. After my initial talks with Bill Shankly had not resulted in my signing for the Anfield club, Liverpool had withdrawn to leave the way clear for Manchester United, and now my decision was made. For better or for worse, I was throwing in my lot with the Old Trafford club. The interlude was over . . . I had made my choice, and only time would tell whether it had been the right decision, or the wrong one.

4   The Reds Get Relegation Blues

Minutes after I had signed for Manchester United, at a Scottish record fee of £200,000, I was being whisked by car from Glasgow, so that my name could be registered with the English Football League to beat the forty-eight hour deadline – and I so nearly didn't make it, because the car in which we were heading south was involved in a crash which could have brought my new career in football to an end even before it had begun. But good fortune on that occasion was on my side, for while the car was badly damaged, I suffered little more than bruising and a shake-up, and was able to take my place in Manchester United's line-up for the game against West Ham at Old Trafford on January 20 1973.

I was yet another addition to United's Scottish clan, for the player squad at Old Trafford included Martin Buchan, Denis Law, Willie Morgan, Alex Forsyth, George Graham, Jim Holton and Ted MacDougall. Tommy Docherty had taken over as United's manager just before Christmas, and he had wasted no time in recruiting new players. George Graham arrived from Arsenal, Alex Forsyth from Partick Thistle, Jim Holton from Shrewsbury, Mick Martin from Bohemians, and myself from Celtic.

That meant an outlay by United of around half a million pounds in a matter of mere weeks, and it took the club's total spending on new players to one million pounds in ten months. Four of the newcomers – Alex Forsyth, George Graham, Jim Holton and myself – were scheduled to play in the match against the Hammers, and I felt that

I had made the right choice, because it seemed clear to me that, desperately though United were in trouble at that moment, they were determined to retain their status in the First Division.

They had given abundant evidence of this, with their heavy investments in the transfer market, and while it is true that money alone cannot command success, I felt that here, surely, was the hallmark of a club which was ready, able and willing to do things in the grand manner. Failure could not even be contemplated.

The programme for the game against West Ham had already been printed, and it showed United's team as follows: Stepney; Young, Forsyth; Law, Sadler, Buchan; Morgan, Wyn Davies, Charlton, Kidd, Graham. When the team changes were announced, my name was among them. Writing in the club's match-day magazine, Tommy Docherty said:

'There is a tough fight ahead . . . I fully realise that although I have achieved a great personal ambition in my appointment as United manager, this is only the beginning. Achieving an ambition might suggest an easing up; far from it. For me it is merely the starting signal for a great deal of hard work to try to bring the success that was the regular hallmark of Manchester United. It's going to be difficult, but not impossible, and this view is shared by the men I have gathered around me to tackle the first hurdle of retaining our place in the First Division.'

And it was indeed a heartening start to my career with my new club, when I scored a late goal which gave United a 2-2 draw against the Hammers.

The League table that morning showed Liverpool in command at the top, with 40 points from the 26 matches they had played – three ahead of their closest challengers, Arsenal, who had played one game more. At the foot of the table lay the unfamiliar name of Manchester United, with a meagre haul of 17 points from their 25 matches. Then came Crystal Palace, with 18 points from 24 games, West Brom, with 19 from 25 matches, and Birmingham, with 19 from 26.

At the end of my first game for United, we had pulled level with Crystal Palace on points, and were only one adrift of West Brom and Birmingham. Palace had lost, the other two clubs' matches had been postponed. And Liverpool? – They had been held to a 1-1 home draw against Derby, so their lead had been cut to two points, because Arsenal had won at Chelsea. Almost 51,000 people watched our game against the Hammers, and they saw a dramatic fight-back by Manchester United, because West Ham went into the lead after only 14 minutes, through 'Pop' Robson, and two goals up inside half an hour, through Clyde Best. It took a penalty goal from Bobby Charlton to get United back into the game, with thirty minutes gone . . . and there were only ten minutes of the match left when I slotted home that point-saver.

The following week, we managed a 1-1 draw at Coventry, and hauled ourselves to fourth place from the foot of the table. West Brom and Birmingham lost, Palace drew at home, and all three clubs lay below us . . . while Liverpool, beaten 2-1 at Molineux, found their lead over Arsenal had been whittled down to a single point. Yes, I kept an eye on the results Bill Shankly's team were getting, as the season went on. After all, I might easily have been playing for a championship medal instead of helping to wage a desperate battle against relegation.

With 29 matches played, United had moved up another place in the table, and while West Brom still propped up everyone else, Stoke had slipped into twenty-first place, with Birmingham and Crystal Palace above them. And Arsenal, with 42 points, had overtaken Liverpool at the top. The Gunners had gone to Anfield and scored a 2-0 victory, while Bobby Charlton was scoring the goals that beat Wolves at Old Trafford, where more than 52,000 fans hailed our win. I shall have something to say about our fans later; but right from the start of my career at Old Trafford, they certainly showed that if support could help United to succeed, then that support was there for the asking.

I was on the mark again when we played Ipswich at Portman-road . . . unfortunately, Bobby Robson's men were in scoring form too, and they rattled four goals past United. Which meant that we slid down to twenty-first place in the League table, while the bottom spot was still occupied by West Brom.

Towards the end of February, while everyone else was fighting it out in League games or the fifth round of the FA Cup, Manchester United could do nothing else but watch from the sidelines; our game, a crucial one against fellow-strugglers Crystal Palace, had been postponed. The next match for us was another vital one – because West Brom were the visitors to Old Trafford, and when they went ahead through Jeff Astle after forty minutes, the signs were ominous for us. But Brian Kidd equalised one minute later, and two minutes after half-time, I scored the winner. So back we went, to fourth from the bottom.

Then came a match against Birmingham, who had been hauling themselves away from the danger zone, and we went down 3-1 at St Andrew's. The goal I scored counted for little, although with seven minutes to go, it gave us a chance of a draw. But a last-minute penalty made it three for Birmingham.

However, we beat Newcastle 2-1 in our next home game, and with 33 matches played, we had moved up to fifth from the bottom, and looked to be in with a very real chance of leaving the relegation places to be fought over by West Brom, Norwich, Crystal Palace and Stoke. We held our ground by drawing 1-1 at White Hart-lane, scored an encouraging 2-0 victory at The Dell against Southampton, then beat Norwich at Old Trafford with a late goal from Mick Martin. Nobody could say that Manchester United were surrendering their First Division status without a fight.

When we drew 2-2 at Stoke on April 14, with just four matches remaining, we were really optimistic about our chances of survival, because that victory took us into 16th position in the table, then we drew at home against our greatest rivals, Manchester City. And although we lost our final game of the season, at Chelsea, we had ensured First Division survival, for between us and relegation there were Coventry, Norwich, Crystal Palace and West Brom. We finished with 37 points from our 42 matches, and Tommy Docherty had justified the claim he had made when he was appointed manager at Old Trafford. For he had said then: 'If United go down, I'll need shooting!' As for Liverpool, they had clinched the championship with an Easter Monday win at Anfield against Leeds, and a no-score draw in their final game of the season against Leicester, to finish with 60 points . . . and the final of the UEFA Cup to come.

They won that trophy, too, and I didn't begrudge them their unique double. Naturally, I spent a few moments reflecting on the might-have-beens, had I signed for them. I could have had a championship medal and a European medal in my first season in English football – and medals were what the game was all about. But I felt that next season could be a much better one for United. Which just goes to show how wrong I was . . .

Arsenal 3, Manchester United 0 . . . that was how the first result in the First Division read, at the end of the matches played on the opening day of season 1973-74. But there were 41 other games to go, so Manchester United were a long, long way from having to stage another desperate battle to stave off relegation. After three games had been played, we even began to think about being involved in the First Division championship battle, because we were seventh from the top, and while we had lost one match, we had won our first two games at Old Trafford. It made a change, also, to see that Liverpool were languishing in – for them – an unaccustomed twelfth place in the table.

With five matches played, however, the balance of power had begun to tilt; Liverpool were third from the top, and Manchester United had slipped down to seven places from the bottom. A home win over West Ham, after a 2-1 defeat at Ipswich, was followed by a scoreless draw at Leeds – no mean achievement – and we also drew 0-0 against Liverpool at Old Trafford. By then, nine games had gone by, and there were half a dozen clubs separating Liverpool, in seventh place, from United.

But we lost at Wolves and at home to Derby, before scoring the only goal of the Old Trafford game against Birmingham, and that winner was a curio, for the scorer of our penalty goal was . . . goalkeeper Alex Stepney. He rather fancied his chance, as a taker of spot-kicks, and had volunteered for the job.

A draw at Burnley, another at home against Chelsea, a 2-1 defeat at Tottenham, a 3-2 defeat at Newcastle – where I scored – and an Old Trafford draw against Norwich . . . then there was a postponement of our derby game against Manchester City at Maine-road. We returned to Old Trafford to share the points with Southampton, then we lost in a five-goal battle at home against Coventry, and went down 2-0 at Anfield.

The turn of the year brought us to the half-way mark in the League season, and we were back on familiar territory – for, reading from the bottom of the First Division, the relegation candidates were spelled out as follows : Norwich City, West Ham United, Birmingham and Manchester United. Three of us had played 22 games, and West Ham had played one match more. Once again, Tommy Docherty's team was beginning to feel the pressure.

New Year's Day was an unhappy omen. For we lost in London just as we had done on the opening day of the season. This time, instead of Arsenal, it was Queen's Park Rangers who defeated us by a clear, three-goal margin. In the third round of the FA Cup, I scored, to give us a 1-0 win at home over Plymouth Argyle, but our precarious League position was our chief concern, for by then, with 23 games played, we had only West Ham and Norwich below us in the table. January 12 1974, was one of those four-point affairs, because we had to visit companions in distress – West Ham, at Upton Park. Billy Bonds gave the Hammers a 1-0 lead, after forty-nine minutes, and Sammy McIlroy pulled that goal back shortly after play had been going for an hour; but with only five minutes left for play, Pat Holland scored the winner, and West Ham moved up to four places from the bottom, while we slipped into twenty-first place, with only 16 points to show for our efforts from two dozen matches. It was turning out to be that sort of a season for Manchester United, once again.

A home draw against Arsenal, and then came the bitter taste of defeat in the FA Cup, against Ipswich at Old Trafford. Kevin Beattie stuck the ball in the net after only seven minutes of play, and that was the beginning and end of the scoring. Now, we told ourselves, the one consolation was that we could concentrate on securing our First Division status – but straight away, as if to emphasise that the fates were not on our side, we went to Coventry and lost.

Sixty thousand people flocked to Old Trafford for the game against Leeds, and they saw Mick Jones and Joe Jordan rub salt into our wounds with goals which sank us firmly to the foot of the First Division table. We were one point adrift of Norwich, and had played 27 matches. Fifteen games to go . . . could we stage another Houdini act?

While teams such as Liverpool, Leeds and Leicester strove to stay on the Wembley trail, when the fifth round of the FA Cup came along, we went to the Baseball Ground to take on third-placed Derby County. Few people gave us a chance of getting some reward from that fixture, but we salvaged a point with goals from Brian Greenhoff and Stewart Houston – after having gone two down. At home, we had scored 16 goals and conceded 15, with five games won, five drawn and five lost; away, we had failed to register a single victory, drawn only three matches, and lost 10 – which meant we had played more games at Old Trafford than away, and on tour had scored only eight goals, while conceding 23 in our 13 games.

As had happened when we drew against teams such as Norwich and Southampton earlier in the season, we failed to score at Old Trafford against the Wolves, and thereby dropped another precious point. But the first Saturday of March gave us a lift, for we went to Bramall-lane, and I scored the goal which gave us a much-needed, morale-boosting victory.

But a couple of weeks later Birmingham, standing only one place above ourselves in the table, scored three minutes from the end of the match at St. Andrew's, and then we lost at home to Tottenham. The last match in March renewed our hopes of escaping the drop, even though we were at the bottom of the First Division, because we gave Chelsea a 3-1 beating at Stamford Bridge. We still had eight matches to play, compared with the seven left to Southampton, Birmingham and Norwich.

I scored the first of our two goals, when we played Norwich at Carrow-road, and we exchanged places at the foot of the table; six games to go, and it was Norwich 25 points, United 27, Birmingham 30, Southampton and West Ham 32 apiece. West Ham, however, still had some cause for concern, because they had only five matches left. When Jim McCalliog scored the only goal of the game at Old Trafford against Newcastle, we had put four points between ourselves and Norwich, and edged to within two points of Birmingham and three of Southampton. It was a cliffhanger, all right . . . and the tension was beginning to show.

Our 39th match of the season was a four-pointer, because

we had to tackle Southampton at The Dell. Weeks earlier, they had looked in no danger of dropping out of the First Division, but some bad results had put them bang in the middle of the relegation dog-fight. Almost 31,000 people turned up for that clash – and as the Saints don't normally command such gates, the significance of the occasion was clear.

When Jim McCalliog stepped up to slot home a penalty with the game barely twenty minutes old, we felt that we could still save ourselves; but Mike Channon scored an equaliser shortly after half-time, so we had to settle for one point, instead of the much needed two. Still, we had three matches left, and were only a point behind Birmingham and two adrift of the Saints. And each of these teams had played 40 games. The First Division lifeline was still dangling tantalisingly within our grasp.

But fate had one final trick to pull, in that topsy-turvy season for Manchester United. And our doom was sealed, even though we still had a couple of matches to play. Norwich were down, Southampton and Birmingham were each playing their final match, and we were going into our 40th game of the season . . . against Manchester City, at Old Trafford. We had to win, to have a chance of staying up.

This was the situation, at kick-off time on Saturday, April 27, 1974: Birmingham were at home to Norwich, Southampton were away to Everton, United were at home to City. Norwich had played 40 games, but had only 29 points; United had played 39 matches, and had 32 points; Southampton had played 41 games and had 34 points; and Birmingham, also on the 41-match mark, had 35 points. West Ham, who had also been involved in the scrap at the bottom, were playing their final game of the season, against Liverpool at Upton Park, and they had 36 points.

After the game at St Andrew's had been in progress for only two minutes, Norwich went a goal ahead. But Bob

Hatton and Kenny Burns each scored in a two-minute spell shortly before half-time, and that was how the scoreline remained, to the end of the match. West Ham finished up by drawing 2-2 with Liverpool, and Southampton sprang one of the shock results of the day by giving Everton a 3-0 hiding at Goodison Park. Normally, that would have been an occasion for celebration, but as the Saints' general manager, Ted Bates, left Goodison with team-boss Lawrie McMenemy, he was heard to observe: 'This is the saddest victory I've ever known.' For he was aware that, in spite of the Saints' final fling, they were doomed to the Second Division.

And what of Manchester United, contesting the derby game before almost 57,000 partisan spectators at Old Trafford? – It was to prove an occasion of drama . . . and complete anti-climax. The atmosphere was electric, as the game began, with the Manchester City supporters making no secret of their ambitions – they wanted their team to apply the coup de grace to United. And what irony there was in the situation, too, for Denis Law, who had reigned for so long as the king at Old Trafford, had joined the Maine-road club for the second time in his career, after having been freed by United at the start of the season.

There had been considerable speculation before the game, of course, about Denis – what if he scored the winning goal against his old club, and thus sent them spinning out of the First Division? – It was a situation which he must have felt keenly, and I know I wouldn't have liked to be in such a position. Or would I? – Once the game begins, remember, you're playing to win . . . and no one had been a greater competitor than the former Manchester United star.

United and City went at it, hammer and tongs, but neither side had achieved a breakthrough . . . until there were only eight minutes of the match still to be played. Then Manchester City struck – and, inevitably, or so it seemed, the player who had to score the goal was . . . Denis

Law. I can still see his face now, after he had tucked that chance away; and I'm sure he felt just as sick as the Manchester United men. It was surely the goal which had given him least pleasure in his scoring career.

There was pandemonium, of course, and the fans began to invade the field. The game was finally restarted, but with four minutes of time officially remaining, the referee felt that he had no option but to call a halt to the proceedings, for the fans were threatening to over-run the pitch, and there seemed no way that the game could be completed without crowd problems. So Manchester United's First Division life came to a premature end, with four minutes of the game that were never played.

But the final twist was that the match might as well never have been started, in any event, and Denis Law did have the consolation of knowing that his goal didn't really send Manchester United into the Second Division. The other results settled it for us – by the time we had completed our programme, we still had only 32 points. And down we went, with Norwich and Southampton.

Like the rest of the United players, I felt sick with disappointment. Sick for myself, sick for the club, sick for Sir Matt Busby and for manager Tommy Docherty. And 'the boss' took it harder than anyone, because in spite of the fact that it's the team which wins or loses matches, he shouldered the blame himself. He felt that it had been his responsibility to maintain Manchester United's First Division status; and he took it hard, when the club descended into the Second Division. 'I'm the man who took Manchester United down,' was his theme; and I know it still rankles with him that it should have happened under his management.

Still, the impossible had happened; United, once the kings of European Soccer, as well as the crack club in English football, had finally been vanquished into the lower regions. I thought once again of Liverpool, finishing second to Leeds

United in the First Division, and going to Wembley to win the FA Cup against Newcastle . . . but you cannot live a life of regrets, and having made my bed, as it were, there was nothing I could do but lie on it.

When the first stages of stunned disbelief had begun to wear off, everyone at Old Trafford got down to thinking and working for a return to the First Division the following season. We all felt that it was the least we could do, if only to give our tremendous supporters something to cheer. They had stuck with us to the end, and we were determined that a few months hence, we would show them that we were not going to become buried in obscurity.

It's easier said than done, of course, and many people in football have made promises in moments of disappointment which, later, they have found they could not keep. But there was no question about the mood at Manchester United. We were going to have a damned good try at bouncing back to the First Division at the first attempt. And in style, too . . .

5   The Changing Face of United

Now, I think, is as good a time as any to take stock of the transition Manchester United have undergone, during the past few years. The European Cup winners of 1968 had seen Sir Matt Busby appointed general manager, and in turn, Wilf McGuinness, Frank O'Farrell and Tommy Docherty had been given the task of following in his footsteps. By the time Tommy Docherty arrived in December, 1972, Sir Matt had become a director of the club and, for the first time since his reign had ended, United had a Scot as manager once more.

On the playing side, there were men who had been among the greatest names in world football: Denis Law, Bobby Charlton – these had been stars during United's triumphs of the past, but their days at Old Trafford were drawing to a close. At the end of season 1972-73, Bobby Charlton, United's team captain, announced his retirement as a player after 20 years' service with the club. He had played no fewer than 604 League games for United, but a few months after I arrived at Old Trafford, he was moving in as manager of Preston North End. And the day came, not so long afterwards, when Denis Law found himself being given a free transfer, and rejoining Manchester City.

By the time season 1973-74 came around, Ted MacDougall had moved on to West Ham, and United's playing staff represented a mixture of the old and the new. Alex Stepney, who had been signed by Sir Matt Busby from Chelsea in 1966, was still there, and his deputy was Jimmy Rimmer, who later went to Arsenal in a £50,000 transfer deal. Still on United's staff was David Sadler, who had arrived in November, 1962, as a free-scoring forward, and stayed to make his name as a defender who was capped by England. Sadler, like that star of England's 1966 World Cup side, Nobby Stiles, eventually moved on to Preston, who also signed Francis Burns from Old Trafford.

Martin Buchan, signed from Aberdeen, had been with United since February, 1972, and Steve James and Arnie Sidebottom, both young defenders who had known only United as professional footballers, were also on the staff. There was an Irish contingent – George Best, Sammy McIlroy, Trevor Anderson – and these players had all been there before Tommy Docherty's arrival. So had Brian Kidd, Peter Fletcher, Willie Morgan, Ian Moore, Tony Young. Tommy Docherty had injected new blood into the squad by signing no fewer than seven players, including myself.

In the same month that I joined United, Mick Martin, a midfield player from League of Ireland club Bohemians, came to Old Trafford at a fee of around £30,000; and in the following April, Bohemians also supplied United with an inside-forward called Gerry Daly, while Shelbourne, another League of Ireland club, provided a left-back named Ray O'Brien. Shortly before my arrival, Tommy Docherty had recruited George Graham, who had been under him at Chelsea, and who had moved on to Arsenal. George succeeded Bobby Charlton as United's team captain.

The Scottish clan was strengthened, also, by the signings of centre-half Jim Holton from Shrewsbury Town and full-back Alex Forsyth from Partick Thistle. Alex had arrived at Old Trafford in December, 1972, and Jim, like Mick Martin, George Graham and myself, had joined United in the first month of 1973. No one could say that Tommy Docherty had let the grass grow under his feet in the few weeks since he had been appointed manager, and charged with staging a relegation rescue act. As time went by, there were other arrivals, too – Ron Davies, the Welsh international striker; Jim McCalliog, who – like George Graham – had been a player under The Doc. at Chelsea; and goalkeeper Paddy Roche, signed in October, 1973, from Shelbourne.

The turnover in talent at Old Trafford was tremendous, during the next couple of seasons or so, as even more players arrived and others departed. One of the unluckiest was undoubtedly winger Ian Moore, who had been signed for a fee of something like £200,000 from Nottingham Forest in 1972, and had suffered severe injury in training the following season, which meant that he missed the last three months of the campaign. Moore, who had won England recognition, found that he could not overcome the injury in the end, and so he had to bow out of top-class football. It was a big blow to player and club, when the final decision had to be made.

The signing of Paddy Roche eventually paved the way for Jimmy Rimmer's departure to Arsenal; and Brian Kidd left Old Trafford for Highbury, too. Steve James moved on to York, managed by United's former team boss, Wilf McGuinness; Willie Morgan returned for a brief spell to his former club, Burnley, before joining Bolton; Tony Young and Trevor Anderson left United, and so did Peter Fletcher, whom Hull City signed as part of the deal which brought striker Stuart Pearson to Old Trafford.

Ron Davies, George Graham and Jim McCalliog faded from the Old Trafford scene, and by the start of season 1975-76, the playing personnel had altered dramatically, from the first days of Tommy Docherty's instalment as manager of Manchester United. Stewart Houston, a full-back from Brentford, was there to partner Alex Forsyth on the flanks of the back-four line, and Brian Greenhoff, younger brother of Stoke striker Jimmy, was staking his claim to a regular first-team place. He started off in the middle of the park, but after Jim Holton had suffered a broken leg, he dropped back to form, with Martin Buchan, United's central defensive pairing. And Tommy Jackson arrived on a free transfer from Nottingham Forest to get a taste of first-team football in midfield.

As time went on, Jimmy Nicholl emerged as a challenger for a place at full-back or in the middle of the field, and wingers Steve Coppell and Gordon Hill were added to the staff, at a total outlay of little more than £100,000. Steve, studying at Liverpool University and playing for Tranmere Rovers, had attracted the interest of quite a few clubs, and the same could be said of Gordon Hill, who was making his mark with Millwall. But it was Tommy Docherty who backed his judgement and took the plunge for both young-sters, and they repaid United's investment handsomely.

So The Doc wheeled and dealed, and players came and went. And the net result was that, suddenly, Manchester United seemed to have a new-look side which offered hope for the future, with a brand of exhilarating football which produced results and gave the spectators full value for their money. I shall have something to say about United's storm-ing promotion campaign later, but as of now, let's take a look at my Old Trafford team-mates.

One or two of the established first-teamers, such as Martin Buchan and Alex Stepney, were not brought to Old Trafford by Tommy Docherty; but it is fair to say that the Man-chester United of today are very much Tommy Docherty's team. Alex Stepney, for instance, was signed by The Doc during his days at Chelsea. Alex cost Chelsea a then world record fee of £50,000, and most people anticipated that his arrival at Stamford Bridge heralded the departure of Peter Bonetti.

In fact, Alex played just one First Division game during his stay of 112 days at Stamford Bridge, and few players can have had such contrasting experiences during their career as the man who now keeps goal for United. His first-team debut was in a match at Southampton, which Chelsea won 3-0; and it was on the return journey, when the Chelsea team stopped for a meal at an hotel in Winchester, that

Alex came to know that Tommy Docherty was a man who could make a spontaneous gesture of generosity. The Doc suddenly appeared with boxes of 50 cigarettes apiece for the smokers in the side. He had paid for the cigarettes himself.

Alex found that having kept a clean sheet at Southampton didn't automatically win him regular first-team football, however, and the day came when Tommy Docherty, who claimed that he had the best two goalkeepers in the country, was even suggesting that Alex and Peter Bonetti should play in alternate matches. Finally, Alex wanted to know where he stood – and The Doc told him. It was a bit of a shaker, too, because Alex learned that inside a week, he was likely to be transferred to Manchester United. He was sworn to secrecy, and asked not to tell even his wife, who was anticipating a different kind of move – into a new house down south.

In the end, Chelsea did transfer Alex, and got their £50,000 back; and Alex went on to claim a European Cup-winner's medal with United. He recalls an occasion when United went to Stamford Bridge and stopped Chelsea – then at the top of the First Division – from taking a clear lead over their championship rivals. The Doc was straight into United's dressing-room afterwards, to congratulate the winners and remind Alex of what he had told him before that transfer to United. 'I said you wouldn't regret the move . . . you've got the best manager in the business there,' said Tommy.

So there were no hard feelings when Alex Stepney and Tommy Docherty linked up again, at Old Trafford. But The Doc produced another shock when, at the start of season 1975-76, he said that Alex would have to give way to Paddy Roche. Alex had played right through United's promotion campaign, but The Doc regarded Paddy as 'the man for the future.' Alex Stepney's reaction was quiet, but firm: 'I'll back my record against his (Tommy Docherty's) judgement,' he said. As it happened, Paddy had to cry off at the start of the season, because of a family bereavement, and Alex stayed in goal.

But not so long afterwards, Tommy Docherty did promote Paddy Roche, even though Manchester United were sitting pretty at the top of the First Division table. Unfortunately for Paddy, things went sadly wrong during the next few matches, and after Alex had carried on doing his job in the reserves, he was reinstated in the first team. Once again, Tommy Docherty made a typically forthright admission, a couple of months or so later, when he said publicly that he had made a mistake in dropping Alex Stepney. And Alex, once back, stayed in the side right through to Wembley.

Alex is one of the quieter guys in the United team, as well as the most experienced. But, being a Londoner, he has a sharp sense of humour, and he has seen it all, during his career, which began with Tooting and Mitcham. He's been through the four divisions, and through the mill, and Paddy Roche has found that it's been a waiting game, by and large, in the reserve team at Old Trafford. Paddy, who joined United in 1973 from Shelbourne, had already been capped by the Republic of Ireland in 1971, and he made two League appearances during season 1974-75, when Alex Stepney was injured, then he had that brief encounter in First Division football the following term, before Alex reclaimed the first-team spot.

Alex played 137 League games for Millwall, that one first-team game during his stay at Chelsea, and by the time the 1975-76 season had ended, he had completed more than 500 appearances in League football and going on for 300 since his transfer to Manchester United. In his first season with United, he collected a championship medal, and in his second, he was a member of United's European Cup-winning side. He knew the disappointment of going down to the Second Division and the pleasure of gaining a promotion medal.

As I said, Alex has seen it all in more than a decade at Old Trafford and elsewhere, and it's not surprising that he is a down-to-earth character who just goes on doing his job quietly, but effectively – even if he does crack on that he doesn't like his wife, Pam, going to United's matches. She went to a couple of games and United didn't do so well, so Alex claimed that enough was enough!

The fact that Alex Stepney has beaten off more than one challenge for the first-team goalkeeping spot, in his years at Old Trafford, speaks for itself. It shows that he has learned his trade well, and that he doesn't quit when the going gets tough. And despite the disappointment of missing out on a winner's medal at Wembley in the spring of 1976 – it would have completed his collection – he had the consolation of knowing that coming up was a testimonial game as a reward for the tremendously consistent service he has given to Manchester United.

Another defender also named Alex – Alex Forsyth – has had his ups and downs since he arrived at Old Trafford in 1972, as well. Alex is a very cool customer on the field, and he is a player with more than his share of sheer foot-balling skill, for although he plays at right-back, he isn't just a stopper. He can take on a man and beat him, and there is nothing he enjoys more than moving forward and having a crack at goal.

I think that this characteristic makes him a player in the traditional Manchester United mould, and he has demon-strated quite a few times that he packs a real wallop of a shot from around 25 yards, as the goals he has scored from this kind of position testify.

But there was a time when he found himself out of the United side, early in season 1975-76, and he had to fight his way back. Jimmy Nicholl, the young Irish lad who is so easily distinguishable by his red thatch, broke through to stake a claim for a first-team place, and Alex was the player who had to drop out, for a spell. It didn't exactly make him happy, but he grafted away until he won back his place. Jimmy, however, still showed that he was a challenger to others, both in the back four and in midfield, and he clearly has a future in top-level football.

Incidentally, manager Tommy Docherty showed that he could play it tough, when he axed Alex from the first team – and it was a demonstration (not for the first time) that reputations didn't guarantee first-team selection. Alex was dropped for a game against Tottenham . . . only three days after he had collected another international honour by playing for Scotland in a European championship match against Denmark in Copenhagen.

The Doc stated his case firmly : 'We have a squad, and the team will be picked from it. I'll make what I consider the necessary changes. Even if we are winning, I shall still make changes when I consider it could strengthen the team.' And he has pursued that policy more than once . . . as I know, from personal experience.

Tommy Docherty could have hidden behind an excuse too, when he axed Alex Forsyth, because the player had returned from the international with a slight ankle injury. 'Out through injury' would have been the diplomatic term used by many a manager; but The Doc made it clear at the time that he had been considering promoting Jimmy Nicholl, in any event.

But United's manager can soften the blow, too, for he pointed out that sooner or later, every player in a team finds himself in danger of losing his place. So far as he was concerned, he could understand a player not liking it, when he was demoted – but it was something he had to accept. At least, on those terms, you know where you stand, and you know that if you do get the chop, the remedy is in your own hands . . . you've got to play yourself back into the side. And it is to the credit of Alex Forsyth that he did just that, after a few weeks in the reserves.

Not surprisingly, his team-mates all know Alex Forsyth

as 'Bruce', although he is not like the famous comedian in build – even if, now and again, he does stick his chin out! If Alex has got one superstition, it's that he likes to carry a football out with him when we go on the field, and in the dressing-room before a game, he and Gerry Daly have a game of their own in which the idea is to keep the ball moving between them without letting it touch the ground.

Gerry was hoping to take a Cup-winner's medal with him when he went home to Ireland to be married, in the summer of 1976, but he was unlucky, in that respect. However, he is still young enough to return to Wembley and finish on the winning side there. You could call him one of the original members of what the fans term 'Doc's Army', for he was given the chance to prove himself and, by the spring of 1974, he had claimed a first-team place as his own. Since then, he has missed a mere handful of games, and while he may look slim and rather frail, he has shown he can cover every blade of grass on the park, and still keep going.

In United's promotion season, he scored 11 goals in three dozen matches – and nine of those goals came from the penalty spot. He revels in his role as United's penalty king, and seems utterly nerveless when he takes a spot-kick. Considering that he cost United only £15,000 when he was signed from Bohemians, he was a 'steal', and he has shown that he can not only live in First Division football, but that he can take command of a game with his ability to read situations and make and take scoring chances. On his day, he is razor-sharp at spotting openings and switching the direction of play – and far tougher than his slender frame indicates.

As you might expect with an Irishman, he is a bit super-stitious, at times – during United's challenge for the title and their run to Wembley, he wore what he called his 'lucky' suit to every match. He is a very good snooker player, and one of his close pals is 'Hurricane' Higgins. Maybe if Gerry hadn't taken up football, he and 'Hurricane' would have been opponents in professional snooker.

We call Gerry Daly 'The Ghost' – for obvious reasons – but the name which has stuck to Stewart Houston is 'Steve Austin.' And with his physique, he is built just like the Six-Million-Dollar Man of television fame. Stewart has graduated from football in the lower regions, with Brentford, to Scotland international recognition, and at £40,000, he was another snip of a signing by United.

Like Alex Forsyth, he has claimed a few goals, and his height and strength make him a tremendous asset as a defender. At one time, he was on the playing staff at Chelsea, and it seemed as if his career had taken a real downward step when he moved to Brentford; but Chelsea's loss has becomes United's gain, and since he claimed a first-team place at Old Trafford, no one has been able to dispute his right to the left-back position.

Everyone knows by now that Martin Buchan is fluent in languages, and that he sings and plays guitar. Few people, probably, know that Martin is the namesake of a footballing father, for his Dad used to play Soccer, although it was mostly as a part-timer in the Highland League in Scotland. Martin junior is a man of many parts; he speaks French, German and Spanish, and when we made a club record at Old Trafford, he did a solo spot on the flip side.

Martin always gives the impression of being a precise individual, who knows exactly where he's going and, perhaps, has what you might call a 'departmental' mind. In the dressing-room, however, he wanders around in shorts, track-suit top – and his shoes and socks. But when he does come to put on his football boots, he gives them an extra polish ... even though they have already been polished by one of the ground-staff lads.

Martin became a professional with Aberdeen in 1966, as a teenager, and during his four years with United he has shown himself to be one of the most accomplished footballers in the game. He is always cool, very quick, and nothing ever seems to ruffle him. Not surprisingly, he became a Scotland international, and was in the 1974 World Cup squad. Many people felt that he was unlucky not to have played in the home-international series of 1976.

The memory that many people will have of Brian Greenhoff is that television shot showing him squatting on his haunches and wiping the tears away with his sweat-stained jersey, after Manchester United's 1976 FA Cup-final defeat by Southampton. Sometimes television captures for all time a moment which the subject of the picture would like to forget – remember England 'keeper Ray Clemence, for instance, letting that shot go between his legs in the Hampden game against Scotland. But Brian Greenhoff need never feel ashamed of shedding tears at the end of the 1976 Cup final; there were a few more of us who had to choke them back.

Neither was it the act of a player who is a bad loser, or a moaner. Normally, Brian is one of the most cheerful characters you could find, but on that occasion, the emotion and the disappointment finally just had to break through. His real character showed, though, a few days later when he picked himself up and played himself into the England side.

Not only that; he shrugged off a ligament injury and declared himself fit to join the England party which went to the United States for the games against Brazil, Italy and Team America. For Brian is a born competitor, and he has to give everything for ninety minutes. His pride in playing for United and for England is very real, and his ability matches that pride.

Brian's elder brother, Jimmy, plays for Stoke, and the two of them are good pals – except when the clubs are in opposition. Then, there is no quarter asked or given. Some people thought that when Brian left school at Barnsley, he would go to Leeds United, as Jimmy did, in the first instance. But Manchester United won the quest for his signature, and he signed professional as soon as he was seventeen. Tommy Docherty would be the first to admit that having Brian already on the playing staff when he arrived was a bonus, because this youngster has all the right credentials for the big-time.

Brian made his first-team debut for United in 1973, against Ipswich, and he has graduated to full England status via the Under-23 side. Recognition came swiftly during 1976, but the lad had earned it. He started his career as a midfield player, but was an instant success when he switched to the back-four line, and while he may not be a giant in height, he reads a game so well, and is so mobile, that very little gets past him.

He's what I call a dedicated professional, too; he's one of the first into the dressing-room before a match, gets stripped and changed, and sits there quietly, waiting for the signal to go into action. I think that during the pre-match spell, he mentally tunes himself for the game, and certainly he is concentrating all the time he's out on the park.

And now we come to the men who have done so much to renew Manchester United's reputation as an attacking team – the forwards. Starting off with Belfast-born Sammy McIlroy, the lad people once dubbed as the new George Best. Sammy broke through to United's first team before I had ever arrived on the Old Trafford scene, but I know, from what people have told me, that he didn't much enjoy the business of people making comparisons so early in his career. It wasn't that Sammy disregarded the tremendous talent of his fellow-Irishman; it was just that he wanted to be allowed to play the game in his own style, and be judged on his own performance.

He won four international caps at schools level before signing apprentice professional forms for Manchester United in August, 1969 – yes, he's been at Old Trafford that long –

and he made his first-team debut in November, 1971, when he was seventeen years old. In one of the toughest matches you could wish, too – a derby game against Manchester City. And he could already call himself a Northern Ireland international, for he had won a full cap against Spain early that year.

Season 1971-72 saw him being blooded gradually in United's first team, and he was expected to make the real breakthrough the following season. But a road accident early in 1973 almost put paid to his career, and it took him some while to regain full fitness. So, in effect, Sammy had to start all over again. But he made it, in no uncertain fashion, and is now a regular choice for club and country. Apart from his ability to beat a man, he has a great talent for poaching goals out of half-chances, and whenever he gets the ball inside the eighteen-yard box there is danger for the op-position. Before a game, he has to endure some kidding from us, though, for he seems to be in a constant tizzy sorting out match tickets for friends and relatives. It's a wonder he has any energy left to play football.

University graduate Steve Coppell is regarded as the 'Mr Brains' at Old Trafford, and there is a constant quiz battle between Steve and his team-mates. It was United's good fortune – and Liverpool's and Everton's loss – that this youngster from Merseyside came to Old Trafford, and his career has a parallel to that of Steve Heighway, for each player went to Wembley in his first full season . . . and each finished on the losing side, too. So maybe that's a good omen for Stevie the second.

Steve got into League football via the Third Division, for he joined Tranmere Rovers, and it wasn't long before he was making his presence felt. The big question, of course, was whether or not he would click if he moved into a higher class of football, and it was Manchester United who, in the end, were prepared to give Steve the chance to supply the answer himself.

Luton manager Harry Haslam tells the story of going to watch Tranmere play – his target was another youngster, but 'everyone thought I was after Steve Coppell.' Harry claimed that Manchester United snapped him up when they heard he was going to Prenton Park, but I suspect that Tommy Docherty would dispute that. Not that it matters, because Steve did arrive at Old Trafford, and United found they had gained a winger with skill and no little amount of courage.

Steve continued his university studies while he was playing football for us, and he still managed to hold down a first-team place, despite the pressures which a bid for the title and the FA Cup inevitably bring. But he took everything in his stride, and I feel certain that he will continue to present problems to opposing defences – and to represent a bargain signing, at £40,000.

Steve Coppell did well enough to attract the attention of England manager Don Revie, and so did two more of United's players who were signed by Tommy Docherty: Stuart Pearson and Gordon Hill. Gordon, who plays on the left flank, cost £70,000 when he joined United from Millwall, and he made an impact almost immediately. He was, said United's manager, the final piece of the jigsaw. 'We are now in a position to play 4-2-4, with natural orthodox wingers who can also score goals. I've always wanted my team to play this way . . . there is a tradition here of open, attacking football.'

Tommy Docherty pointed out that Gordon Hill was the first really true left-winger at United since the days of David Pegg and Albert Scanlon. Ian Moore, whom the manager described as 'more of a roving forward', might have got his chance to fill that left-wing vacancy, but the injury he received finally put him out of the reckoning. So Gordon was recruited, and with Steve Coppell on the right, and Sammy McIlroy and Stuart Pearson in the middle, United had four genuine attacking forwards – plus the backing of myself and Gerry Daly, and the adventurous flair and scoring opportunism of men at the back like Stewart Houston, Brian Greenhoff and Alex Forsyth.

Gordon had played in American Soccer the previous summer, with Chicago Sting – the club managed by a former United star, Bill Foulkes – and he made a hit in the U.S., averaging almost a goal a game in the twenty-two matches he played, and finishing up the second-top marksman in the U.S., Soccer League. On his return to Millwall, he scored eight goals for the London club, before signing for United. And his strong finishing, especially with that lethal left foot, his pace, courage and readiness to take defences on made him an exciting proposition for United. Gordon is a cheerful, bouncy character, too, who never had any doubts about his ability to move into top-grade Soccer and become a success.

Derby won't need to be reminded about the two goals he hammered past them in the 1976 FA Cup semi-final – yet he is honest enough to be self-critical, too, for after he had been substituted in the final against Southampton, he declared that he had had 'a stinker.' Personally, I felt that he was being too harsh on himself, although I know he was judging himself by the extremely high standard he sets.

We call him 'Merlin', and you don't have to be a magician to realise that he has bamboozled plenty of opponents since he burst upon the First Division scene. He hasn't done so badly in his England career, so far, either. He's quite a card, and he gives us many a laugh when he does a 'take-off' of famous people in the world of show business. Close your eyes, and you can easily imagine that you are listening to Frank Spencer, of the famous television comedy series, or to Norman Wisdom, Max Bygraves or one or two other top showbiz personalities. But 'Merlin' cuts out the clowning when he dons the red jersey of Manchester United; for Soccer, to him, remains a serious business, and he is very ambitious to make the greatest possible impact in the game – and at the highest level, which means in international football.

Gordon's arrival meant that a free-transfer signing by Tommy Docherty was squeezed out of the first-team scene, if only temporarily. Tommy Jackson, who won Northern Ireland international honours as an Everton player, had arrived from Nottingham Forest, and he did a really valuable job for United, before Gordon joined us. Later on, he was to show that he could still do a useful stint in the middle of the park. The Doc described Tommy once as 'a model professional', and he has shown on many occasions that he echoes the spirit of the new United. He's a team man, and he wants the team to do well.

When players such as myself have been out of action through injury, Tommy has come into the side and given his usual, ninety-minute performance, and I know that he feels he's achieved an ambition in itself merely by being asked to join Manchester United. Over and over, The Doc has gone to some lengths to stress the importance of team spirit, and the fact that these days, a player-squad is essential. 'Players have got to accept tough decisions with the professional attitude of Tommy Jackson,' he once summed up.

Another player who has had to accept the role of substitute is an Irish teenager by the name of David McCreery. David appreciates that he is young enough to make a forward position his own for years to come, eventually, but in the meantime, he has had to settle for being the guy who played a waiting game. He got into the side during my absence through injury, and when Gordon Hill came off in the FA Cup final, it was David who got his chance of playing at Wembley. He can make goals and score them, and if he looks a baby-face, you can take it from me that he shows not the slightest trace of being overawed once he goes into action. He keeps other players on their toes, too, because they know he's lurking in the background – and it's not surprising that he's become known as United's super-sub.

So now I come to the last name on my list, concerning United's strike force – Stuart Pearson, who arrived from Second Division Hull City in exchange for £170,000 and forward Peter Fletcher. In the spring of 1976, Stuart graduated to full England international status, when Don Revie's team toured the United States, and I have the feeling that he could well be wearing the No.9 jersey in the 1978 World Cup – assuming that England qualify.

I suspect that England manager Don Revie sees in Stuart one of the main candidates for a place in his line-up, over the next few years, and while our front-line striker is a broad-shouldered, strong lad, just watch how quickly he can move to turn round defenders, and how much sheer footballing ability he possesses, with those subtle flicks and feints. He's not just the old-fashioned type of bustler, although he can use his weight; he's a genuine all-rounder, like most of his team-mates.

Stuart arrived at Old Trafford towards the end of my first full season there, and possibly there were people who wondered if he would rise to the occasion, after having had only Second Division experience. Tommy Docherty recruited Stuart after United had been relegated – it was his one and only major signing, as he set his sights on steering United back to the First Division straight away. In our relegation season, we had totalled only thirty-eight goals, which was United's poorest scoring record in their post-war history. Stuart Pearson was the man The Doc felt could pep up the scoring rate again, and lead United's attack with flair.

With Hull, Stuart had scored forty-four goals in 126 games, and during United's promotion campaign, he was our leading League marksman. When we reclaimed a First Division place, he had to prove himself all over again, and he did have a spell – who doesn't? – when the goals were simply not going in. That lean spell lasted more than a couple of months – Stuart scored twice against Sheffield United in mid-December, and didn't get another goal until he netted against Derby towards the end of February. Naturally, he did his share of worrying during that bleak period . . . but when he scored against Derby, his old confidence came back, and he rattled in four more goals in the next half-dozen matches.

By the time we were coming towards the end of the 1975-76 season, I was leading the way with fifteen goals in League and Cup, and Stuart had chalked up a dozen goals. The previous season, he had scored seventeen League goals, and I had scored eleven – plus, I hasten to add, seven in the League Cup to Stuart's one. Sammy McIlroy was on the mark a dozen times when we came back into the First Division, and Gerry Daly – admittedly, with the help of a few spot-kicks – reached double figures, too. So you can see that in the Manchester United side of today, the scoring is really spread around.

It's as well to remember, also, that Stuart Pearson has had his share of injuries, or he might well have scored even more goals; and he has had to take a lot of stick from uncompromising defenders. Maybe that's why he goes through such a rigmarole before a game, such as having a quick bath, then getting the physiotherapist to apply oil to his legs and shoulders and, finally, strapping his ankles to ensure that they have extra support.

They say that the strength of a club is only as good as its reserves. Well, Manchester United have now built up a strong squad of players, with Paddy Roche and Ray Mountford – an England youth goalkeeper – as cover for Alex Stepney. Jimmy Nicholl I have already mentioned, and another youngster, Arthur Albiston, has been blooded in First Division football, too. He's a natural cover for Stewart Houston at left-back. United have Jim Holton, of course; they could switch Stewart Houston into the middle of the back-four line; and Steve Paterson, a teenager from north of the Border, can be looking towards his chance of first-team outings before too long.

Standing 6ft. 2in. tall, and weighing 13 stone, Steve is the right build for a back-four player, and he almost got his big chance in season 1975-76, for when United played Leicester in the fifth round of the FA Cup, there was a danger that Martin Buchan would have to cry off, and Tommy Docherty was all set to plunge Steve into the action. It would have been a big test for a lad aged seventeen, but United's manager would have had no qualms. One of the greatest centre-halves Scotland ever produced was called Willie Woodburn and, according to Tommy Docherty, Steve could become Woodburn the second. United took a strong fancy to the boy when he played for the Scotland youth side at Old Trafford – and now he's one of the 'clan.'

In midfield, United have the promise of youngsters like Tony Grimshaw and Jimmy Kelly, and Jimmy is another of the Scottish brigade at Old Trafford. Again, he is still only in his teens, yet he was made substitute for one of our First Division matches, which shows how much faith the manager has in him. Jimmy is a Scottish youth international, although he hails from Carlisle, just south of the Border. Up front, there is a lad called John Lowey, who was allowed to further his experience by playing in American Soccer during the summer of 1976. When United went on tour to the United States and Bermuda, John was in opposition to his Old Trafford team-mates . . . and he scored the two goals which earned his side a draw.

Even further down the assembly line – and I'm talking in terms of youth – there are other lads working for the chance to make the grade at top level. Former Yorkshire schoolboy player Paul Smith, signed at fifteen, is one; he can play in midfield or in attack.

We have a lad from Blackheath called Gary Micklewhite, who plays in midfield; a Welsh youngster named Martyn

C

Jones, who is a centre-back and played for Glamorgan schools; another youngster, Dave Haggett, who has skippered the Welsh schoolboys; a lad by the name of Andy Ritchie, from Stockport, who showed his paces as a striker, when he played for England boys against France, in a game which was televised from Wembley; while Bootle boy Steve Jones is an England trialist. So there is plenty of up-and-coming talent waiting to break through at Old Trafford – youngsters whose names, as yet, are unknown to the vast majority of football followers, for the most part; even those, probably, who so fervently support Manchester United. But one day some of them could become household names in First Division (and maybe international) football.

I have referred more than once, in passing, to United's 'new look' team, when talking about the players who have seen the club through from the Second Division to the First, but it is interesting to reflect that although we sprang so swiftly to the forefront of the First Division, once pro-motion had been assured, there is a tremendous leavening of experience right through the side. Stepney, Forsyth, Houston, Greenhoff, Buchan, Macari, Daly, McIlroy, Coppell, Pearson, Hill . . . all have collected representative honours. Tommy Jackson is a Northern Ireland international, Paddy Roche has been capped by the Republic of Ireland, and David McCreery has come to the notice of the Irish selectors.

So, while Manchester United may have brought back the art of playing with 'old-fashioned' wingers and using the whole width of the pitch, giving our football a new and exciting appearance, I can say in all honesty : never mind the width . . . just look at the quality. Tommy Docherty has certainly wheeled and dealed, signed and sold; and I believe that, in the end, the unanimous verdict will be that he has also delivered.

For we're his team; the team The Doc built. Make no mistake about that. And we shall all sink or swim together. I firmly believe that we shall swim, especially after the lessons we learned the hard way during our relegation season, our promotion campaign, and our return to the First Division.

6 Who Really Knows The Doc?

Who really knows Tommy Docherty? – There's a bit of Bill Shankly in his make-up, a touch of the Matt Busby, a glimpse of the showman, now and then. There's a touch of the tyrant, on occasion, plenty of generosity at other times – and the whole of the mixture adds up to a man of complexities and contradictions. Yet through it all there shines one element which can never be denied. First and foremost, and evident above everything else, Tommy Docherty is a man whose heart and soul are in football.

The Shankly touch? – That was apparent, when Manchester United met Derby County in the semi-final of the FA Cup, and The Doc summed up, after having taken a look at the star-studded opposition. He told the United players that Derby were the ones who were doing the worrying. All the advice he had to give to his own team was contained in this simple sentence: 'Go out and enjoy yourselves.' The United players took Tommy Docherty at his word, and ran rings round the opposition.

The Busby touch? – That was apparent when the final whistle went at Wembley, and The Doc immediately turned and hugged his opposite number, Lawrie McMenemy. Manchester United's manager must have been choked with disappointment, like his players, but he managed to conceal his innermost feelings, as he congratulated the manager of the opposition. He could feel for his players, too, as he showed when he walked across to Brian Greenhoff, who was kneeling on the turf, a picture of dejection, and gave the young United player a consoling pat on the back. As Brian rose, and began to walk off the field, Tommy Docherty walked with him, his arm around Brian's shoulder.

Later, after giving Southampton full credit for their victory, in a television interview, Manchester United's manager went the whole hog and telephoned his congratulations to the Saints, at their celebration banquet. It must have cost Tommy Docherty a lot to make such a gesture . . . yes, there was a touch of the Matt Busby, all right, about that.

The touch of the showman came before the final, when The Doc went on television and, in answer to a question as to which was the top manager of the lot, he looked the camera straight in the eye, and gave himself the vote. ' I think I am, at this moment,' he said.

Tommy Docherty has expressed the opinion that he isn't happy unless he's talking. And he has had plenty to say about the game, and people in it, during his time as a player and as a manager. By the same token, plenty of people have had a considerable amount to say about the man everyone calls The Doc – although not always to his face. And I dare say that he doesn't need to be reminded that a few eyebrows were raised, when his appointment as the manager of Manchester United was announced.

Like myself, Tommy Docherty has never been afraid to accept a challenge; otherwise, he wouldn't have stopped off at Chelsea, Rotherham, briefly at Queen's Park Rangers, at Aston Villa and in Oporto, on his way to becoming United's manager. The fact that he was already making a success of the job as Scotland's team manager didn't deter him from taking up the challenge at Old Trafford.

He knew that at that moment in time, it was just about the hottest seat in football, and a lesser man might have first quailed at the prospect, then found a very good excuse for staying put. But The Doc had no hesitation, and sometimes I wonder if the major factor which influenced his decision was his high regard for Sir Matt Busby. Remember, he had once told Alex Stepney, after having transferred him to United, that he was playing for the best manager in the business.

Tommy Docherty had long been noted for expressing opinions which were controversial, to say the least. He was known throughout Soccer as a character – and a man of direct action, when he felt the occasion demanded it. In his days as the manager at Chelsea, Ron Harris had called Tommy Docherty a man who was in a hurry, a man who wanted a short cut to success. The Doc signed and sold many players in quick succession, as he was later to do at Old Trafford. He sent some of the Chelsea men home from Blackpool, after they had broken curfew – and, perhaps, was astounded at the publicity which that bold move generated.

Generally, Tommy Docherty gave the impression that wherever he was, there would be sparks flying . . . and, maybe, there would be a love-hate relationship between himself and some of the players under his command. They tell me that during the war, an American general named George Patton made his name as a man of quick decisions; The Doc could indeed be regarded as the 'Blood-and-guts' Patton of football.

In 1967, the year that Glasgow Celtic won the European Cup, Tommy Docherty steered Chelsea to the final of the FA Cup at Wembley. He had signed Tony Hateley as a £100,000 striker, and when the big fellow scored the goal which put Chelsea through to the final, The Doc openly proclaimed his delight, as he hugged Tony Hateley and told the world: 'That's what I paid £100,000 for!'

Almost ten years later, Tommy Docherty was scoffing at those who tried to tell him that Wembley was a jinx ground, for him. 'I'm not superstitious,' he declared firmly. Yet after Southampton had won the Cup, Manchester United's manager must have begun to wonder if, indeed, someone up there didn't like him, for he had by then recorded seven visits to the famous stadium, without a win to his name.

Four times he had been there with the Scotland team – and never been a winner. He was a player with Preston, when they lost the 1954 FA Cup final against West Brom; and in 1967, as the manager of Chelsea, he saw his side defeated by Tottenham. Nine years later, and he was the manager of a beaten Manchester United side. Yet he told anyone who cared to listen: 'If they call it a jinx to keep on getting to Wembley, let me be jinxed year after year . . .'

Ten years have passed, since Tommy Docherty and Alex Stepney parted company at Stamford Bridge, and a lot of water has flowed, since then, as they say. George Graham and Jim McCalliog, two other internationals who came under Tommy Docherty's management, also parted company with him, renewed their acquaintance briefly at Old Trafford, before moving on once more. And other former Manchester United players have reason to remember the impact he made upon them and their careers, both at club and international level.

Denis Law was one man to whom The Doc gave a free transfer; George Best was another. Willie Morgan, who had shared some great moments with Tommy Docherty at international level, and been promoted to skipper the team for a spell at Manchester United, finally returned to Burnley at a fraction of the price United had originally paid the Turf Moor club for him. Bobby Charlton's retirement, as The Doc himself admitted, solved a problem which, in the end, might have become embarrassing for player, manager and club. And Tommy Docherty has never made any secret of his belief that when he arrived at Old Trafford, there was a weeding-out process he felt had to be done.

The playing side was not his sole concern; changes eventually took place on the backroom staff. John Aston, who had once been a player for United, and seen his son a first-teamer there for a spell, left the club – he was duly rewarded for the great service he had given United – and Paddy Crerand, after a spell as Tommy Docherty's assistant, was allowed to leave and pursue his own managerial ambitions. Tommy Cavanagh became the first-team trainer, and Frank Blunstone, who might have become the manager at Chelsea, chose to throw in his lot with The Doc and United. He arrived as the youth-team coach, and shortly after the 1976 FA Cup final he was appointed assistant manager.

At the start of The Doc's career at Old Trafford, there were cynics who felt that maybe he wasn't quite United's style. Sir Matt Busby had been so much the diplomat, the man who preferred the velvet-gloved approach, even if the glove did occasionally reveal an iron fist. The Doc was volatile, voluble and, at times, abrasive. A contrast in many ways to the man who had guided Manchester United to the pinnacle of Soccer success during the 1960s.

When Manchester United slipped through the trap-door into the Second Division, the cynics were swift to forecast that there would be rumbles of unrest among the players, who had been so used to the glamour that they wouldn't settle for second-best. Well, I'll admit that the prospect of visiting Second Division outposts of football didn't exactly set me afire with excitement . . . but, like my team-mates, I stayed, and we got on with the job. So did Tommy Docherty, despite the suggestions from the cynics that, after his spending spree and United's failure to survive as a First Division force, the writing was on the wall for their manager.

Some of the cynics hedged their bets, by declaring that things would be all right for The Doc, so long as the team was going full-steam ahead for the First Division again; but if Manchester United showed that they were nothing better than a middle-of-the-table side, then Tommy Docherty could beware, by Christmas. But Manchester United repaid the faith of their fans, and confounded the cynics, by doing very nicely, thank you, once they had accepted their role as a Second Division club – temporarily, that is.

They spent just one season in Division 2, and raced away with the championship, so that the doubters were forced to think the whole thing out again. The doubters hadn't quite finished, because they came up with another answer – that gaining promotion was one thing, especially when there were so few top-class challengers in the Second Division; but staying the pace in the First Division would be an entirely different kettle of fish.

Amid all the speculation, however, Tommy Docherty maintained a low profile, on the whole. As he admitted later, even he did not know for certain how well-equipped his side was to withstand the pressures which would undoubtedly be applied by the likes of Liverpool, Leeds, Derby County and Queen's Park Rangers.

Yet, as season 1975-76 went along, The Doc showed on occasion that there was still fire in his belly, as he came up with one or two outspoken comments. He gave Birmingham a bit of a slating, for the way he claimed they had played at Old Trafford – and then apologised for his remarks. He didn't agree with a former Manchester United player, Johnny Giles, who – after a distinguished career with Leeds – was in charge of West Brom and the Republic of Ireland international side.

United had agreed to let Mick Martin go on loan to West Brom, and finally the transfer was made permanent. Mick, in fact, played a big part in helping West Brom return to the First Division. In the meantime, he was chosen regularly to play for his country, while Gerry Daly was going along merely to sit on the substitutes' bench. And the Doc didn't like this, and said so. He argued that it wasn't doing Gerry's morale any good, sitting it out as a permanent substitute for the Republic, and he threatened to refuse to release Gerry, if this situation continued.

The Doc had signed both players, and he demonstrated

his loyalty to Gerry, just as he demonstrated his loyalty to Martin Buchan, when it came to selection for the Scotland international side. It is a fact, as I know personally, that Tommy Docherty can differ with you on one thing, and still give you his full support on another, and Martin and he had not always seen eye to eye about things, in their time at Old Trafford. Tommy Docherty and I haven't always seen eye to eye, too, but that's another story.

The Doc incurred the wrath of some people north of the Border, when he said he believed that Martin should be in the international side, instead of Tom Forsyth. United's manager was virtually accused of trying to pick the Scotland team, as well as his own. So The Doc and others have differed. And among 'the others' I have to include myself.

The first year or so of my career as a Manchester United player fell a long way short of expectations, and what I had hoped to achieve with the Old Trafford club. Apart from the problems of fighting to avoid relegation, I experienced some personal low moments, as I struggled to find the form which had made me an international and a regular first-team player with Glasgow Celtic.

There was no doubt in my mind, either, that I was being asked to undertake a role which did not suit either my temperament or my style of play, for United wanted me to play as an orthodox centre-forward, and I had no illusions as to the impact – or lack of impact – I was making. Quite simply, I knew that it was a lost cause, as I tried to pit my five-foot five-inch frame against the towering defenders, in a direct confrontation.

This wasn't the role I had enjoyed with Celtic, and I felt that it restricted me from doing what came naturally – buzzing around, working out things for myself during the course of a game, and nipping in to score goals. I did tuck some chances away, but I knew, without needing to be told, that this wasn't the Lou Macari for whom Manchester United had paid such a great deal of money.

I knew that as the months went by, people were asking how United had come to splash such a huge fee on me . . . and there were those who, no doubt, declared that Bill Shankly and Liverpool had had a lucky escape. You know, even when there are thousands of people packing a ground such as Old Trafford, you can still catch the odd shout from the crowd – especially when it's directed at you; and away from the action, I could sense that the people who supported United were not exactly hailing me as a hero.

My nature is such, however, that I react to insults concerning my professional skill by becoming even more determined to show that my detractors are wrong. Once upon a time, I had heard it said – in my schoolboy days – that I was probably too small to make my mark in English football.

Now here I was, a highly-priced professional footballer with one of the top clubs in England, and things were going far from right for both of us. It took many months for me to achieve real recognition, and a change in style which allowed me more freedom, but in the end, I succeeded. Although it wasn't before I had almost ended my career at Old Trafford.

Tommy Docherty and I had come to know each other pretty well, I thought, from the days when we were virtually neighbours together in Scotland. The Doc used to visit my home fairly often, and I felt that he had a healthy respect for my footballing ability; likewise, I had a high regard for his knowledge of the game and his influence as a manager, especially when I played under him for Scotland. But meeting him a few times a year for the games in which Scotland were involved was different from being under his command day by day, at club level.

And as the time passed at Old Trafford, it seemed that the great hopes both of us had had were doomed to failure. I discovered that he could be really hard, when he felt the occasion demanded it, and stubborn, when he believed he was in the right. So can I, because in many ways I have the same sort of temperament as United's manager. And, looking back, I think I can honestly say now that in our moods of yesteryear, a clash of personalities was inevitable.

Such a clash occurred in the October following my transfer to Manchester United when Tommy Docherty felt that I wasn't doing my stuff in the first team, and he dropped me from the side. I turned up at United's training ground one morning to find that I was expected to train with the youth team, and that, to me, was like adding insult to injury. At Parkhead, everyone had trained together, and after a career at the top, I didn't go much for the heavy-handed treatment.

United were scheduled to play in a game at Mossley, and they were turning out a side which was composed virtually of the youth-team players. On the afternoon of the game, my telephone rang at home and Tommy Docherty informed me that I would be playing at Mossley that night, against the Cheshire League side. I was more than stung – I was furious. And I didn't bother to hide my feelings, as I said that there was no way he would find me getting stripped to play in what I regarded as an insignificant game. I wasn't getting at Mossley, but I felt deeply that I was being humiliated by the order to play.

So we bandied words on the telephone, and Tommy Docherty grimly warned me that if I persisted in my refusal to turn out, there could be only one sequel : he would speak to the chairman, and recommend that I should be fined two weeks' wages and put on the transfer list. That didn't deter me, and I slammed the phone down; then I picked it up again, and rang Cliff Lloyd, the secretary of the Professional Footballers Association. I explained exactly what had happened, and sought his advice.

Cliff Lloyd has done a tremendous amount for footballers, and he knows all the answers when there is a dispute such as this. And the answer he gave me, in calm and measured tones, was that I would be out of order if I maintained my stubborn attitude. Cliff is the sort of man who can bring the voice of reason to bear, most times, when his advice is sought, but I wasn't in the mood to be reasonable, and although he said that Tommy Docherty was within his rights, I replied that there was still no way I would be playing at Mossley that night.

When I had finished speaking to Cliff Lloyd, I sat and brooded; and then I began to cool down; and then I began to realise that what he had said made sense. This was one battle I wasn't going to win.

So I decided that I would go to Mossley, after all, and I travelled on the team coach with the youngsters. I was sitting in the dressing-room when The Doc turned up. I was waiting to see what United's team was, and he was obviously shaken to find me sat on the bench, for he hadn't travelled on the coach so, presumably, he had expected that I would be marked absent. And knowing me, he had already spoken to the chairman before setting off for Mossley, and explained that it looked as if I were digging in my heels.

Tommy Docherty just looked at me, as I sat there, and told me straight to my face that I was being transfer-listed and fined two weeks' pay; and I met him head-on, saying 'Fair enough', then marching out of the dressing-room. When I got outside, it was pouring with rain, and it was bitterly cold, and I wondered what the so-and-so I was doing, and how it would all end. That particular episode ended with my getting a lift back to Manchester in a car belonging to a Pressman – yes, the newspapers knew all about the Macari rebellion, and that was the sort of story that made headlines.

There were one or two more interviews between the United manager and myself – the storm didn't blow itself out straight away – but gradually we both cooled down to the point where each of us was prepared to see reason and act sensibly. Perhaps, in a way, that episode completed a part of our Soccer education for both of us; shouting and losing our tempers at each other didn't do anything for individuals or for the club. And the club had problems enough, as it was. So my name was taken off the transfer list, and I was reinstated in the first team.

There was another occasion when I was axed from the side, later on, but this time I reacted in a totally different manner. The Mossley incident had taught me that there were times when you simply had to swallow your pride, especially if you knew, deep down, that the other guy had the law on his side, as it were. I admitted to myself that I had not been the sensation of the year at Manchester United, and once I faced up to that, the rest followed naturally.

I buckled down to the job of proving that I could win back my place in the first team, and retain it on merit. I accepted that my name and reputation were not sufficient to guarantee a successful career at Old Trafford, no matter what I might have achieved at Glasgow Celtic, and I worked it out that a policy of playing it cool and getting stuck into the job of grafting for a first-team spot was the only one that would pay dividends. It did – and so did United's acceptance that I could never succeed if I felt tied to a role which simply did not suit my style of play.

I was given my chance to do what I enjoyed most. Instead of playing to orders as a target man up front, I was allowed to work things out for myself, within the framework of the team, as had been the case when I was with Celtic. And from that moment, we were all happier. Gradually, the name of Lou Macari came to mean something to United's supporters, and it gave me a feeling of warm pleasure to know that people who had once dismissed me as a bad buy were singing my praises. And as the fans came over to my side, I began to repay them with the sort of football which had brought me success earlier in my career.

I also have to admit that I have profited from some advice which George Graham, a fellow-international, offered me before he left Old Trafford. George had been around, and was experienced enough to know what was what in Soccer; he had served under Tommy Docherty at two different clubs, and probably knew him as well as anyone. George told me that there could be only one boss at a club, and that was the manager. He had to make the decisions, and whether you considered them right or wrong, he took the responsibility. When I thought about this, I realised that George was right.

I had spent a fair amount of my time at Manchester United fighting The Doc, trying to prove that I would not be browbeaten or made to feel that I was being bossed. But I came to terms with the situation, and I recognise now that while a player and his manager may often agree to differ, only one man can make the ultimate decision, and that decision will be made because the manager believes it is in the best interests of the club he is serving.

So Tommy Docherty and I have learned to live with each other, and I hope and believe that out of our misunderstandings of the past has been forged a far healthier respect for each other. The Doc isn't a man to bear grudges – he'll come straight out and tell you to your face what he thinks, and he'll issue the orders . . . but if he finds that you are ready to accept his decisions, after having said your piece, then that's fine by him.

And my acceptance of this relationship has helped to cement a new and better understanding between the pair of us. So much so, that The Doc was plugging for me when the Footballer of the Year poll came along in the spring of 1976. When I didn't win that award, he even said he wouldn't attend the dinner in London!

Yes, Tommy Docherty can give absolute loyalty to his

players, when he feels they have earned it, and no one can deny that he is a players' man, through and through. And at the end of season 1975-76, when Liverpool's Bob Paisley claimed the Manager of the Year award, I was delighted for United's team boss when he won the divisional award.

I mentioned earlier that Tommy Docherty's heart and soul are in football, and they tell me that during his days at Chelsea, he would think nothing of going out training, getting bathed and changed, catching a plane to Scotland to take in a night match, flying back from Glasgow at midnight, and being back in his office by 8.30 the next morning. Well, he hasn't changed a bit. He's still perpetual motion, still ready to talk football into the wee small hours; still ready, as well, to watch a game of football every night of the week. In short, he's a Soccer fanatic – and, in my book, one of those people who are good for the game. And when you look back to the time you thought you hated the guy, that's quite an admission for anyone to make.

I know that The Doc is fired with the ambition now to make Manchester United THE greatest club in the land once more, and I, for one, wouldn't bet against him doing it. For a start, United have that tremendous reputation which has brought them fans – and fan clubs – not just throughout the length and breadth of Britain, but around the world. Coaches arrive regularly for games at Old Trafford from London, Wales and other points north, south, east and west. And the massive support which United have maintained through the bad days and into the good days once again makes it certain that the club will be able to compete with anyone, if Tommy Docherty feels a certain player can strengthen the side.

Players and supporters generally tend to keep their eyes on the ball, as it were; what concerns them is the on-field action, and the results the team achieves. As Manchester

United have demonstrated time and again, over the past 30 years, football is big business in so many ways, and while every manager is judged on his team's performances and results, it should not be forgotten, either, that these days especially, the manager of a Soccer team has far greater responsibilities than merely picking his side for Saturday's match.

A manager must be an astute businessman, as well as an expert on the game; and when it comes to assessing Tommy Docherty's qualities in this direction, I think he graduates with honours, too. He has never been one to jib at spending hundreds of thousands of pounds on one player – Alex Stepney, Tony Hateley, Stuart Pearson and myself are examples of signings where The Doc set records or splashed huge fees. But Manchester United's manager has been prepared to invest modestly, and even in the free-transfer market, when he has decided a certain player will fit into his scheme for the team. And he has sold just as shrewdly as he has bought, on the majority of occasions.

In the summer of 1976, Chelsea's plight made headline news, when it was announced that the Stamford Bridge club was more than two million pounds in the red. Chelsea's problems, in the main, were caused by the erection of a magnificent new stand, which was a costly business, especially when it came to paying interest on the money borrowed, and by the club's descent into the Second Division, for the gates fell to the point where they didn't enable the club to break even. I'm sure Tommy Docherty felt a pang or two of real sympathy for Chelsea, when the news broke; after all, he had once been their manager.

In his days as the team boss at Stamford Bridge, when Chelsea were making a bold bid to land the League championship and the FA Cup, The Doc was one of the biggest spenders in football; but he certainly balanced the books, when it came to adding up the outlay of cash and the intake. Tommy Docherty took over as Chelsea's manager in

September, 1961, and in the space of just five years, he paid a total of £368,000 on new players for the Stamford Bridge club; but he also raked in £544,000 from the sale of players – so he could point to a profit of £176,000, overall. I'd say that was a pretty fair record, especially as Chelsea got the taste of European football, made an appearance in the final of the FA Cup, and went close to winning the championship of the First Division.

What has all this got to do with Manchester United? – Well, in some ways I think there is a parallel. While United were struggling so desperately to retain their First Division status, they spent heavily on new players, and the spending continued when Tommy Docherty arrived on the scene. In fact, there was a time when Manchester United were more than half a million pounds in debt, and even the greatest club in the business has to draw the line somewhere. United had a double worry, indeed . . . their battle to ensure survival in the First Division, and the huge amount of money which had to be paid out in interest. Tommy Docherty's task, for all his freedom to invest heavily in new talent, was to get the club on an even keel, football-wise, once more, and to bring to a halt the drain on cash resources.

One of the essential ingredients, of course, was that the support should remain constant, and United had good cause to be grateful to their vast following, during those days which caused so much anxiety for the players, for their manager . . . and for their directors.

Obviously, when players such as Denis Law, Tony Dunne and George Best were given free transfers, and when Bobby Charlton retired, the wage bill was lightened to a considerable extent; but it was still a drop in the bucket, compared with the tremendous overheads the club had to face. The successful season in the Second Division was something for which United could indeed be thankful – and so was the shrewd selling of their manager, as he raked in much-needed cash for players who were transferred to other clubs. United may not have sold anyone for a quarter of a million pounds, but they got some useful money in for several players, and the result was that the club finished up by making a profit of almost £165,000.

Once we had regained our place in the First Division, it was far smoother sailing, from a financial point of view, as well as on the playing side. The team that went to Wembley in the spring of 1976 had cost around £800,000 to assemble – and of that total, Tommy Docherty had been responsible for spending something like £650,000. But he had also raked in a considerable amount of money from sales, and the results the team achieved continued to draw the supporters in ever-increasing numbers.

By the time Manchester United kicked off in season 1976-77, the club was anticipating a profit of around quarter of a million pounds . . . and the take from season-ticket sales added up to half a million pounds, a record figure for any club in British football. So in two years, United had recovered from their worst-ever financial situation to be hailed as the millionaires of Soccer once again, in just about every respect. From being half a million pounds in debt, they were in the black – and very much so. It was an achievement of which the club could be proud; and Tommy Docherty was entitled to his share of the credit, for team performances, and for the healthy financial situation. The clouds had rolled away, and there was the silver lining.

No one felt the impact of United's relegation more keenly than their manager, and I believe that the mere fact of taking the club back into the First Division acted only as a spur to him. What United achieved in their first season back in the top flight was fine . . . a bonus, if you like, because no one really knew what to expect . . . but Tommy Docherty is single-minded in his ambition to make that just a stepping-stone. He will not be satisfied until his team have been hailed as the outstanding side in the country, until the honours have come to Old Trafford both in the domestic competitions, and from abroad.

And I'm one of the people who go along with that ambition, for I believe sincerely that Manchester United are equipped in so many ways to scale the heights. We have the stadium, we have the support; and we haven't got a bad team, either! But perhaps most important of all, United have the ambition and the will to restore the glory of former years, when they were the toast of the nation. And Tommy Docherty, the man who is at the helm now, is a team boss whose horizons are boundless. From now on, failure is a word which won't even be contemplated, either by the club or by their manager. And like The Doc, I hope to be there when the Reds go marching in!

7 'Little Louie'
by Manchester United manager TOMMY DOCHERTY

Manchester United have a footballer called Lou Macari, and a chairman called Louis Edwards. They provide quite a contrast, because the chairman is a big fellow, and the footballer stands around five feet five inches tall. Whenever I see the two of them together, it's not surprising that I think of them as 'Big Louis' and 'Little Louie.' And I feel sure that neither of them will mind me telling you that . . . because it's the prelude to a story which, I think, demonstrates quite clearly that while Manchester United are a club with plenty of class, there is no class distinction at Manchester United.

Any way, the chairman went to the races one day, to see a horse which he owned – by the name of Three Sevens – running. By coincidence, Lou Macari went to the race meeting on the same day. Naturally, both chairman and player were hoping that their luck would be in. The chairman's horse failed to win its race, however . . . but the player, who had backed another gee-gee, happily collected his winnings.

So what happened, when 'Little Louie' met 'Big Louis'? – The player commiserated with the chairman about his horse having failed to win, and then said: 'Never mind – come on, we'll still celebrate out of my winnings.' And Lou Macari treated the chairman of Manchester United to a bottle of champagne, over lunch, that day.

Sometimes, on match days, I hear someone saying: 'Good luck, Louis.' When the players hear it, they turn to each other and ask: 'Does he mean Big Louis or Little Louie?'

That's the kind of cheerful atmosphere we have at Old Trafford – and I hasten to add that usually we do win.

So now I'm going to stay with 'Little Louie', and give you my impressions of Lou Macari. As I said in my foreword, I felt at the time I signed Lou Macari from Glasgow Celtic that he was more a player for the future, even, than for the present. This was because he was still only in his early 20's, and I believed that time and experience would see him mature into a great footballer. I wasn't wrong in my assessment, either . . . but it took quite a while for me to get the formula right.

To be perfectly honest, I was looking at Lou Macari as a goal-scorer; and there is not the slightest doubt that he has the knack of tucking away scoring opportunities when he gets inside the box. However, although I felt that he was one of the few players from north of the Border who would fit into English football straight away, we both found that we had to work on it. Lou was sharp and quick, and great in the box – there was never any doubt about that. But I came to realise, in the end, that I was the one who had made a mistake in my calculations.

Once Lou had joined Manchester United, I played him up front; but as time passed, it seemed that he wasn't the same player I had known in Scotland. And we both realised this. Eventually, I had to agree with him . . . the mistake I had made was in not realising that he was better GOING into the box than simply BEING in the box. So it was agreed that Lou would operate more in midfield, and that it would be up to him to weigh up when to get into the box for a chance of tucking the ball away. Lou knew his game, all right, and once I was ready to accept that, he became a different player and we were all much happier.

He has won over all his critics, and I'm delighted for the boy. I'm still very much 'the boss' – and I always will be, I hope – but I have to say, too, that Lou will still chip in with his opinion, when he thinks that something needs to be said, and I'm ready to listen to him, as well. Lou is by no means a 'yes-man', and that quality has been to the benefit of the team more than once. He is a great talker on the field, and not above telling someone else how he can improve his game. Lou genuinely wants to help his team-mates, and when he tells someone to do a certain thing – or to stop doing it – during a match, it's because he really feels this will be best for the player and for the team.

If Lou decides, in the end, that he is banging his head against a brick wall, he'll drop the matter and get on with his own game. But I might say that now there are very few occasions when a team-mate doesn't heed the advice given by Lou Macari. Although HE isn't always right, either.

In those early days, when I thought he was better playing up front, he disagreed with me and said he thought he should be playing a midfield role, and getting into the box when he reckoned – perhaps by sheer instinct – that a goal was on. Well, we tried it his way in a game at Blackpool, during our Second Division days . . . and he never looked back. OK – so I was wrong. But I was right when Manchester United played Wolves in an FA Cup replay at Molineux during season 1975-76 . . . and this time Lou was gracious enough to hold up his hand.

We couldn't do better than draw with Wolves, in the first game at Old Trafford, and when we went to Molineux, it wasn't long before we were trailing by two goals. I'll admit that I took a gamble in playing Lou, because I knew before we kicked off that he wasn't 100 per cent fit. But that was how important he had become to the side. Yet at half-time, I had no option but to tell him that unless he competed more with Wolves' Willie Carr, who was bossing the midfield for them, Manchester United would be out of business.

Lou agreed with me . . . but with the second half five or

ten minutes old, I realised that we still weren't getting a grip on things. So I brought Lou off, reminding him of what I had said at our half-time team talk. I wasn't blaming him, because I recognised that he had been trying to overcome an injury handicap; but the state of the game and the situation in which we found ourselves simply dictated that something else had to be tried. Lou didn't argue the toss, though. 'You're right,' he said. 'I shouldn't have started the game, in the first place.'

Lou Macari has matured, during his years with Manchester United. When he first arrived on the English Soccer scene, he was inclined to be a bit fiery if anyone argued with him, if someone played it rough on the field, or if refereeing decisions went against him. He was inclined to flare up and show that he was annoyed, to put it mildly. Some people might say, somewhat wryly, that Tommy Docherty used to be a bit temperamental, too, in days gone by . . . and in some ways, I suppose Lou and I are alike. We're certainly both restless guys, for neither of us cares much for the idea of sitting around doing nothing.

On match days, as Lou has said, he's usually the last one in the dressing-room. If he hasn't been chatting to friends at the official entrance, he'll have been watching the racing on television. Then he'll come into the dressing-room maybe 15 or 20 minutes before kick-off time, and get ready for the game, so that there is no hanging around. In this respect, as I say, Lou and I are alike; and these days many people would also acknowledge that both of us have matured.

Lou now accepts decisions and gets on with the game, and I have instilled the need for this into every one of the players at Old Trafford. It's a tremendous credit to Lou that he has overcome the struggles of his early days at United, that he has matured and come to accept that sometimes the verdict will go against him. That doesn't mean to say he always agrees with the verdict, as I know from personal experience – when you ask Lou Macari for his view about something connected with Soccer, you get an absolutely honest opinion. You might not like it . . . but in that case, you shouldn't have asked.

There's many an occasion when I've been handing out advice during a half-time talk, and – if it's involved the midfield section of the team – I've turned to Lou and asked his opinion. And in return, he's said: 'That's all very well – but don't you think that if I do that maybe Gerry Daly can do so-and-so?' I'll argue the toss a bit, especially if I'm convinced I'm in the right, and Lou will still be saying, at the end: 'Well, you asked what I thought, and I've said my piece . . . but you're the boss, so it's up to you.'

Sometimes, I have to say afterwards: 'Sorry, Lou – I was wrong.' At other times, he'll come up to me and say: 'Yes, you were right.' We've ironed out our differences, and learned, as Lou himself says, to respect each other. And in the long run, it's all been for our own good, and for the good of the team. Which reminds me . . . Lou Macari, although a man of definite opinions, is very much a team man, and he has been a tremendous help to the younger players. He's popular with his team-mates AND with Tommy Docherty – although there is still the odd occasion when I have to say to him: 'There you go again . . .'

But, of course, if he didn't have that spark in his make-up, he wouldn't be Lou Macari, and he wouldn't be the player the Manchester United supporters have come to admire. He may crack on that he's not utterly dedicated to the slog of training, but I can say without any fear of an argument that he never shirks, whether it's in practice sessions or in big matches. He would not know how to 'swing the lead.'

As for fitness, he's what I would call a freak – and I really mean that in the most complimentary sense. For a start, he doesn't drink and he doesn't smoke – which gives him a head start. He's also what I call a natural athlete. He carries no spare flesh, and he doesn't put on weight even during the close season. He could knock off for the summer at the end of April, go on holiday, come back home – and turn up at Old Trafford on the first day of the new season as fit as a fiddle, ready to go straight into a First Division match, even without the pre-season training. And I mean that. Which doesn't mean he gets the all-clear to skip the pre-season slog, I should add!

If I had to put my finger on the quality which outshines any other, so far as Lou Macari is concerned, I would say simply that he loves playing football. Tactically, I sometimes suspect that he isn't all that bothered . . . certainly, although my briefings at times are of the five-minute variety, before United go out to play, I've often got the impression after I've been talking only a couple of minutes that Lou Macari's attention is beginning to wander. What HE wants to do is cut the cackle and get on with the game.

One final thing. I mentioned that Lou is a great practical joker, and I know that whenever we are waiting around an airport or an hotel, one or other of the players will be paged to answer a telephone call, or something else will happen. I know, also, that the instigator will have been Lou Macari – in fact, the other lads have caught on to him now, more often than not. And now and again, he gets caught out himself – this happened when we went on a pre-season tour to Denmark, and he discovered that the guys responsible for the joke were a couple of Press lads.

Lou took it all in good part, as he always does; but he got his own back, all right. I still don't know how he managed to do it, but he made sure that everything they possessed – clothes, passports, money – remained hidden. They never saw their belongings from the day they arrived at the hotel until the day they left.

Eventually, Lou produced a piece of paper on which there were the signatures of many 'witnesses', to say that the offenders had suffered sufficient punishment, and that there would be no further retribution when we all got back to England.

Offhand, I don't recall 'Little Louie' having got the better of me yet, but I think it would appeal to his sense of humour to know that his manager can be handled just like any other guy, now and again. So I'll finish with this story about myself. I returned from the club's tour of the US and Bermuda in the summer of 1976 and my next stop was Malta, where I attended a function organised by the local branch of the Manchester United supporters. We all had a great time, too – until I got thrown into the swimming pool. I was fully clothed, and when I came up, gasping for air, I realised that my paper money was floating around in the water. Fortunately, everyone helped to pick up the pieces, as it were, and the notes suffered no lasting damage, once they had dried out. I've no doubt Lou would have enjoyed the spectacle, had he been there.

So now I've had my say about Lou Macari, and I hope that you – and he – have enjoyed reading it. We've fought, but in the end, we've come to accept that our motives are for the best, and we can agree to differ and still remain good friends. I hope and believe we both have a real future together at Manchester United . . . and that brings me back to where Lou Macari left off. So carry on reading what Lou has to say about the club – and about the people inside and outside Old Trafford.

8   Football Is About People

Results are what count in football; but at the end of the day, football is also about people. Managers and officials, players and supporters. And the three people who have had the greatest influence on me in professional Soccer are my father, Jock Stein and Tommy Docherty. I have gone into some detail already about The Doc; so now I'd like to tell you a bit more about Jock Stein, and about my father. I'm not the sentimental type . . . I don't wear my heart on my sleeve . . . but I'm not ashamed to admit that my Dad, who died several years ago at the early age of 47, was very close to me, especially where football was concerned.

Professional footballers don't usually dwell on the physical ailments which can afflict people, if for no other reason than that they, like other sportsmen, are constantly involved with the business of being in peak condition: and cancer probably is the last thing you would expect me to be writing about, in any part of a book dealing with Soccer.

It is a dreaded disease, and it can be a very ugly one; but it is the disease that killed my father. His death left a gap in my life. For ever since I was 13, my Dad had watched me playing football, and given me every encouragement. Indeed, he never missed a game in which I played, almost up to the day of his death, and when I look back, I acknowledge that my Dad's presence on the touchline, on the terraces or sitting in the stand was a real incentive for me. I went out to play for my Dad, because I knew he was there, somewhere in the crowd,

The incentive was simple enough; no one likes to hear the people around him saying his son can't play – and I was determined, in every game, that my Dad wouldn't have to suffer the hurt and embarrassment of listening to remarks directed at me. The folk around him wouldn't know he was my father . . . but I wasn't going to give them the chance to pass comments which, while they didn't realise it, would have been wounding to him. So I was always aware that Lou Macari had to do his best – for his own sake, and for his Dad's sake.

I knew six years before my father died that he was suffering from cancer – indeed, the doctors called me in and, when they had given their verdict, they added that they didn't expect my Dad to live more than three or four months. But the months turned into years, and you can believe me when I say that many a time, I had to choke back the tears as I saw him wasting away before my eyes. We didn't talk about his illness much; my father kept on going to the matches to see me play, and I kept on going out with the idea of making sure that I did him proud. I hope and believe I succeeded, for I know he was proud of what I had achieved, by the time he died. There were times when I could tell, without his needing to utter a word, that he was in agony; and on occasions I tried to ease his pain by giving his legs a massage.

I can vividly remember one day when I asked him: 'Do you want me to give you a rub-down?' I could tell that he was suffering a great deal of pain . . . but when I began to massage his legs, I was shocked, as I saw how the flesh had simply rolled away. A short time later, he was dead. But almost to the end, a matter of mere weeks before the inevitable happened, he still insisted on going to the game to watch his son play. And I'm not looking for sympathy when I say that I feel sure you will appreciate why my father had such an influence over me, and why, especially in those closing days of his life, I was getting on with the game and doing everything in my power to ensure that he could remain proud of my footballing achievements.

If it hadn't been for my Dad, I doubt if I would have become a professional footballer; if it hadn't been for Jock Stein and Glasgow Celtic, I would probably never have made it to the top, and become a player for whom Manchester United were prepared to pay £200,000. It was while I was at Parkhead, and under the influence of the Celtic manager, that I learned right from wrong in football. Despite the fact that I parted company with the greatest club in Scotland, I still like to think that I never had any trouble with Jock Stein, and he never had any with me. He was the manager who instilled into me the proper professional attitude – how to live right and remain superbly fit, for example. As a teetotaller and a non-smoker, I like to think that this self-discipline will add two or three years on to my top-class career.

It was Jock Stein, also, who showed me that the best attitude is simply to go out and play, and remember that football is a game to be enjoyed by the participants, as well as by the spectators. And when you reflect that Celtic won the European Cup, and have been Scotland's most successful club for many years under the guiding influence of the big fellow, it must mean something.

My attitude remained the same, when I crossed the Border – I get bored with listening to talk of 4-2-4 and 4-3-3 – and I'm happy that, in the end, Manchester United and I agreed that my way was best. I don't like hearing a coach telling a defender to mark someone tightly, just because the opponent has a reputation for scoring goals; my footballing creed is that you shouldn't be concerned simply with stopping your rivals . . . you've got to be positive and creative yourselves. If YOU'RE not doing anything about setting problems for the opposition, then you're not really playing Soccer, as I understand it. If you like, Manchester

United showed, on their return to the First Division, that they were a team of silly kids who wanted to play football the way they had done in their days at school – with whole-hearted enthusiasm and enjoyment, a fair share of skill, and giving the sort of entertainment value which delighted the spectators.

Jock Stein always wanted Celtic to entertain, too, as well as win the championship, the Cup and the League Cup each year. But he is a canny fellow – he knows the game from A to Z, make no mistake about that. And he is meticulous about preparation for a game. He doesn't win matches for Celtic by telling his players how to do this or that, but he does know all about the art of ensuring that his footballers are properly trained, so that they are raring to get into the action – and for me, his greatest asset is that he has the knack of being able to pick the right man for the job, especially when things are not going maybe just as they should.

He can also find the right words to spark a player into producing something extra – I've heard him tell a player at half-time 'If that's the best you can do, then you're as well off getting stripped and into the bath.' The player concerned would go out for the second half determined to show Jock just what he could do – and often as not, he'd prove the match-winner.

Jock is a great psychologist. I've heard him mention, in the hearing of a referee who maybe hadn't been doing too well during the first half of a game, that a referees' supervisor was at the match. This little reminder would put the official on his mettle. Most managers think that the game is won between three o'clock and twenty minutes to five on a Saturday afternoon, but Jock Stein prepares thoroughly for those 90 minutes right the way through the week, in so many different ways. He's interested in his players not just during the hours of training, but when they're away from the ground. He knows what's going on all around him, at any given moment, and his players sense this awareness by the manager.

I believe that Jock Stein would have taken English football by storm, had he chosen to leave Parkhead and accept any one of the managerial offers which, undoubtedly, must have been made to him through the years by clubs south of the Border. He would have introduced entertainment into English football at a time when the game was almost grinding to a halt, in this respect.

People in England may tend to dismiss Scottish clubs in general, and Scottish players, but had Jock Stein moved to England, and been able to sign players such as Jimmy Johnstone and wee Willie Henderson in their prime, I believe he would have made people here sit up a bit. He would have introduced attacking football years before it eventually did begin to arrive, with teams such as Manchester United leading the way.

Possibly only one thing would have hampered Jock Stein, south of the Border – the fact that players at English clubs might have found his brand of discipline hard to take, in one respect. I'm not saying that players in the English leagues lead fast lives, but I am saying that at Celtic, the accent was on real dedication – and in no uncertain terms.

Jock's brand of discipline before and after a match was unchanging. When you were away, you didn't get even one drink, and bedtime was at 10 o'clock sharp. After the game, you were allowed to go out – but everyone had to be in by 1 a.m. And the big fellow was always ready to remind you that 'we've got a game on Saturday.' He isn't a killjoy, but he is a perfectionist, and in his book, this means doing everything right and everything possible to ensure that when the match kicks off, no one can be faulted on the score of fitness and effort.

If the result doesn't work out right, occasionally, that's something else – you can't win 'em all. But if Jock Stein gets a second chance, even with that, you can bet Celtic

Golden goal in the F.A. Cup-tie against Peterborough. Full-back Alex Forsyth turns attacker, and blasts home United's opener.

Arm upraised, United striker Stuart Pearson (centre) acclaims his goal against Norwich City, while his team-mates express their delight.

That's my boy! Steve Coppell congratulates Lou Macari, after the little Scot had scored an equaliser against Coventry City at Highfield Road.

It's agony for Birmingham goalkeeper Dave Latchford, as Lou Macari runs in to put the ball into the net.

One that didn't count . . . Steve Coppell's free-kick beats Liverpool 'keeper Ray Clemence — but Lou Macari is ruled offside.

Champions! Manager Tommy Docherty's expression indicates his delight, as fans salute United's return to the First Division.

The two faces of Lou Macari . . . in action for Glasgow Celtic and for Manchester United. Arm upraised, Macari acknowledges the thrill of being a two-goal hero at Molineux, in a game against Wolves which signalled United's return to the First Division.

Manchester City's Mike Doyle and Lou Macari go for the ball, and in this tussle, the City Man is the winner, for Joe Royle fastened on to the flick from Doyle to score against United.

Wembley . . . and United are on the attack. Southampton 'keeper Ian Turner saves a shot from Gordon Hill (extreme right).

It's a goal — or is it? — Sammy McIlroy lobbed the ball goalward, and Lou Macari tried to make sure with this spectacular header . . . but the ball went over the bar, and Oxford gained a reprieve.

Here's a goal from Stuart Pearson, in United's 3–1 victory over Arsenal, which sends the Old Trafford club back to the top of the First Division. And there's no doubt what Stuart's team-mates think. Stuart had a double reason to celebrate because he had just learned of his call-up to the England squad.

Let-off for Spurs, as a goalbound shot from Lou Macari is blocked by Don McAllister.

The fifth round . . . and after Lou Macari had opened the scoring for United at Leicester, Gerry Daly got into the act with this effort. Sammy McIlroy and Lou Macari race up to congratulate Gerry, and United are through to round 6.

It's there . . . Gordon Hill (far left) slots in the first of his two goals against Derby.

Celtic manager Jock Stein pictured here with the shield presented to them for winning the league six times in a row.

will do better in the replay. And somehow, as I said, he can pick the right words or the right man to give his team the required lift.

My outstanding memory of my whole professional career remains my first Scottish Cup final. It was – inevitably – against Rangers, and there were 120,000 people packing the ground, after the first meeting had ended in a 1-1 stalemate. I was just 18, and my name was listed among the squad, but I was utterly certain that the manager had included me just to give me a taste of the big-time, even though I had made occasional first-team appearances. But when he read out the team, at our hotel, I learned I was in the side. I could scarcely believe my ears, and even as I rode in the team coach to the game, I kept telling myself that there would be a lot of other disbelieving faces, when the team was announced to the waiting fans at the ground.

At the same time, I knew that Jock Stein had made a habit of springing surprises – and winning strokes – so something told me that I wasn't going to be a failure that night. I thought to myself, 'I'm going to get something' . . . and I scored one of the two goals which won the Cup.

My respect for Jock Stein is undiminished today, and my respect for Tommy Docherty has increased, as we have come to understand each other. There was a time when it looked like the interests of Jock Stein and The Doc might clash, and I was the man in the middle. It was when Tommy Docherty was managing the Scotland team, and he wanted four of the Celtic players to make a trip to Brazil, for a mini-World Cup tournament. But the tourney was taking place very close to the time when Celtic were getting ready for the new season, and the Parkhead boss called us in and – reminding us of this fact – suggested it would be better if we stayed home.

My three team-mates were not too fussy, and they didn't argue the point. They accepted Jock Stein's advice, and

D

decided against going. Then the Celtic manager turned to me and asked: 'What about you, Lou?' I didn't hesitate. 'I want to go,' I said promptly. Jock, of course, was concerned about the possibility of his players receiving injury which could have ruled them out of the early-season games, and his first duty was to the club. I realised this; at the same time, I felt that it might be my one and only chance to travel to Brazil, to get a taste of what Soccer meant out there. For all I knew, I could be hurt in Celtic's first match, and my career could be over within days of the new season having started.

So I was determined to go, for the trip and for the experience, and quite honestly, I don't think the Celtic manager ever really expected any other answer from me. When I had said my piece, he didn't attempt to try to dissuade me; he simply said: 'If that's how you feel, then go ahead.' And there were no hard feelings on his part. He understood my motives. I played in Brazil against Yugoslavia, we drew 2-2 . . . and I scored both the goals. We lost 1-0 against Brazil, but overall, I learned something from the experience.

As Scotland's team manager, Tommy Docherty wanted to assess every player he possibly could, and the tournament in Brazil gave him useful information – about his own men, and about the foreign sides we met. And it has to be admitted that the loyalties of an international team boss and a club manager must conflict, at times. It has to be said, also, that a manager cannot do it all on his own, and Jock Stein and The Doc would be the first to agree about this. At Celtic, Jock Stein had Sean Fallon as his right-hand man; at Old Trafford, The Doc has a couple of experienced men to augment the backroom side of things. So now let me introduce you to another Tommy – surname Cavanagh.

If there's one character who is football-crazy, it's 'Cav.' Many a time since I joined Manchester United I've thanked my lucky stars I got used to pushing myself to the limit in training when I was with Celtic – because Tommy Cavanagh doesn't wrap things up when he's got you where he wants you . . . working your guts out. It's no secret that not every player is enamoured of the rigorous training schedules which form a part of their everyday lives; it's no secret, either, that Tommy Cavanagh isn't always the pin-up boy at Old Trafford, because he is so enthusiastic – dedicated is a better word – that he pushes you to the extreme, at times. And his Scouse accent is very much in evidence, when he's giving the orders.

'Cav.' gets so involved with football that when he's at work, he just hasn't time to laugh and joke; he takes the game as seriously as anyone I've ever known – and more seriously than most. I think his idea of heaven would be to get up in the morning and spend every day doing nothing but training or talking about Soccer until it was time to go back to bed. And if some of the players feel at times that they almost hate what he's doing to them, well . . . he knows it's for their own good. And they respect him.

Tommy Cavanagh isn't one of the younger breed of trainers; he's been around a long time, and he's been through the mill, in just about all the divisions. He knows what it was like to be a player in the days when the money was comparatively insignificant, insofar as it paid the rent and the grocery bills. Maybe that's one big reason he appreciates the value of things today. And while you can have a laugh and a joke with him off duty, you don't take liberties, and you don't make cracks about the game that brings you such a good standard of living.

Tommy Docherty and Tommy Cavanagh have known each other so long they can almost read each other's minds. In front of the players, 'Cav' doesn't contradict The Doc – but I feel sure that when they are together, he will be ready to express his own viewpoint, even if it doesn't always agree with the manager's. And I have no doubt that Tommy

Docherty has a deep respect for Tommy Cavanagh's knowledge, even if he doesn't always accept his opinions.

There is a third member of the Old Trafford backroom staff who deserves a mention: Frank Blunstone, who has a great deal of responsibility for guiding the young players at the club. Frank is a nice guy, and exactly the right type of person to bring on the youngsters. You can see they are enjoying their training sessions under him. Frank clearly has a great sense of loyalty, too, and he appreciates the loyalty that Tommy Docherty and Manchester United showed to him, early on in his association with the club. For he had barely been appointed when he was badly hurt in a car crash – yet United kept the job open for him until he was fit again. Not so long ago, he could have taken his chance to become a manager at one of the top clubs, but he stayed at Old Trafford. So that loyalty has worked both ways.

Frank has the right ideas, too, about getting the best out of youngsters, from what I have seen. He encourages them to move around, to get into the game and not worry too much about which position they're supposed to be playing. There's nothing worse than to see a lad standing around and out of the game, just because he thinks he's a left-winger and nothing is happening in his section of the field. At Old Trafford, the young players are expected to give it a go all the time – and that way, they can develop an adaptability which, on occasion, surprises even themselves.

Being a professional footballer these days, I suppose, is something of a status symbol, in a way, because so many people idolise their favourite teams and even individual players – although, now and again, the fans can be extremely critical, and express the view that a certain player's brains are all in his boots. But footballers DO have brains, and in recent years we have seen university graduates make the grade in professional Soccer. Steve Heighway and Brian Hall, for example; and our own Steve Coppell. They have been absorbed and accepted into the game, and their team-mates recognise that they have intelligence – because their team-mates are intelligent themselves. The ones who haven't got brains won't make a success of their own careers, and the ones who possess above-average intelligence go on to become world-class players. Take it from me, football is NOT a game for dummies.

In my early days at Old Trafford, I found that Bobby Charlton was one of the most conscientious and hard-working players, and his attitude was reflected in the way he did his training. Brian Kidd, now playing for Manchester's 'other' team, was a good trainer, too. I must admit that I'm still trying to work out what made George Best tick. Frankly, he baffled me.

There were times when George would do things which made you think he had taken leave of his senses, and times when it was crystal-clear he was nobody's fool. Towards the end of his career with Manchester United, after his retreats from and his brief comeback into football, you could see that he was getting caught in possession of the ball, because he had lost some of that pace . . . but he still had so much skill, it was almost uncanny.

At a guess, I would say he finally decided he didn't enjoy the routine of football any more – the training, the graft, the self-discipline. Possibly he looked around and saw people in other walks of life, including show business, who didn't have to apply themselves so much in the purely physical aspect of keeping fit to stay on top of their jobs. I just don't know.

What I do know is that many people still don't realise the tremendous self-discipline a professional footballer must endure, if he is to stay on top. It's a game which demands not just instinctive ability, but loads of energy and stamina – and you don't get that without putting in a great deal of hard work, and making sacrifices when it comes to the social side of life. The footballers who put everything into their career can keep going when others have had to quit – and I hope and believe that my own way of life will see me still going strong when others have bowed out.

Every footballer who has hit the top has had to prove something – to himself and others – during his career. Yes, there's always pressure of one kind or another. In my first few months at Old Trafford, when things were most definitely not going right for me, I knew without being told that I wasn't the most popular player with the fans. There were times, in fact, when I thought of moving on; not because I had lost confidence in my own ability, but because I felt that it wasn't going to be my scene, after all.

Deep down, I knew I could play just as well as I had ever done, but I began to get the feeling that it might take a move to convince people about this. At the same time, I still wanted to be successful with Manchester United – and that thought kept me going. I got through the bad patch, and things started to happen for me and for United. Towards the end of season 1975-76, people were beginning to acclaim me, and I knew I had won the battle, because it had been my best season in English football.

Yet, in the end, it turned out to be the worst, from a personal point of view. I was in the running for just about every award, and it seemed that so many people expected me to be a winner somewhere. I know you always have to try to avoid banking on honours, but footballers are like anyone else – they get excited at the prospect of winning things.

I was excited about my chances of being named Footballer of the Year, the player's Player of the Year, winning medals in the League championship and the FA Cup – and then I was out of action for several weeks through injury, and I saw all my hopes beginning to fade. In the end, it was just too much for me, as I finished with nothing, except a loser's medal at Wembley. At one stage, I even thought I was going to miss the Cup final. But I had to accept the disappointments, and I've got over them now.

When I look back, I have to smile – even if it's somewhat ruefully. In my first full season with Manchester United, we were relegated, and for a player like myself, who had never really known failure, it was a galling experience. I thought of the people in Scotland who might well be saying: 'It serves him right for leaving Celtic.' For I knew I hadn't been popular with the Parkhead fans when I left. As for the Rangers supporters, they would be laughing their heads off at my personal misfortune.

Half of the people in the city of Manchester – those who supported United's rivals – would be quietly smiling, too; and maybe on Merseyside there would be some Liverpool fans who were smugly viewing my own troubles while applauding their team's achievement of winning the League championship and the UEFA Cup. Yes, it was a downhill time for Lou Macari, and I felt pretty dejected by it all.

But you have to learn to live with failure, as well as success, and I still believed that Manchester United were a club big enough eventually to climb back to the top. Tommy Docherty summed it up when he told us, after relegation was certain: 'Well, there's work to be done – we're going to go up again next season.' And fortunately, we all made his forecast come true.

Oddly enough, although promotion was achieved so swiftly and in such a convincing manner, when it finally came, I didn't feel anything. After the last home match, when we had thrashed Blackpool and made sure of finishing as Second Division champions, the players did a lap of honour round Old Trafford . . . yet in a strange sort of way, I felt embarrassed, and couldn't get to the dressing-room quickly enough. I wasn't being disrespectful to our supporters – it was just that I felt deep down that promotion to a club of United's standing wasn't such a great thing. Sure, we had beaten a few good teams on the way, but Manchester United should always be capable of beating opposition from a lower grade, and the Second Division had not really been our place, any way.

After the FA Cup final, I was choked. I tried to hide my feelings, although I felt like crying. You don't want to show yourself up in front of your fellow-professionals, and I was supposed to be one of the more experienced players in the side. So it was up to me to set some sort of example.

In fact, when I looked around the dressing-room at some of the younger players, it seemed to me that they hadn't really taken in what being beaten in a Cup final at Wembley meant. I don't mean that they didn't care – sure, they were so clearly disappointed; but somehow, they seemed numbed. They may have been suffering from the shock of it all; they may even have been overwhelmed by merely having appeared at Wembley . . . I got the impression that some of them were too new to the Wembley scene to have realised exactly what had happened to them, that afternoon. Sometimes football can hit you that way, even when you've won. I'm certain of one thing, though: the next time these players go to Wembley for a Cup Final, someone will suffer for that defeat inflicted by Southampton!

And talking of suffering, I must confess that London is the place where I least like to play. We lost at Wembley, and we don't seem to be able to do much on other grounds in England's capital city. Up to the start of season 1976-77, I had never finished on the winning side, whenever United played in London. The No.1 jinx ground is Highbury, where Arsenal always seem to give us a hammering. I'm not thrilled about playing at Loftus-road, either, for Queen's Park Rangers usually get a result against us; as for West Ham and Spurs, we often seem to draw there when we should really have won. I'm not superstitious, but I can't help wondering if there is a London hoodoo on United.

Mind you, there are other grounds on which it seems we can't go wrong. If London supporters think we're the worst team in the country, and wonder how we've managed to do so well in the League, the fans of clubs such as Aston Villa, Burnley and Norwich City have cause to feel that we make them suffer, because we usually manage to get a result against their teams. We can be hopeful of some reward at Elland-road, these days, too – which reminds me that there are a couple of fans from the Yorkshire area, and one from London, who don't appear to care very much for Lou Macari.

During ninety minutes on a Saturday afternoon, you get used to hearing the roar of the crowd, and sometimes you become the target for a few home truths from the fans on the terraces. The three characters I have just mentioned carry on their feud after the game has ended, for among the mail which arrives for me at Old Trafford are three letters, almost week by week, from the 'I hate Lou Macari' brigade. Not one of the letters contains a signature, so I just have to go by the postmarks; but the message is invariably the same. I'm referred to as 'a stupid Scot who has crossed the Border', and taken to task for having ventured my opinions. Well, freedom of speech is still one of the things left to us.

The one time I did expect to get some abusive letters, nothing happened. I had done a television interview before the Scotland-England game at Hampden, in the spring of 1976, and stuck out my neck by predicting an England victory. After Scotland had won decisively, I half-expected an uprising of the clans . . . but all I got was one solitary letter telling me I had picked the wrong team. Maybe my fellow-countrymen couldn't afford the stamps, at their present price! Any way, I never did expect to get letters from Rangers' supporters . . . they just wait until I return home on a visit, then stop me in the street to tell me what they think about me.

Somehow, while talking about people, I seem to have wandered back to Scotland, so it might interest you to know if there is any difference between derby games north of the

Border, between Celtic and Rangers, and between Manchester City and Manchester United. And the short answer is – yes, there is. Now I'll try to explain why this should be so.

In Glasgow, the fanaticism of the fans for one team or the other stems partly from a religious basis. Rangers are the exclusively Protestant club; Celtic are the Catholic club – although Parkhead raises no barriers against players who are of other religions. So, while every Rangers player is a Protestant, Celtic's side is often composed of players whose religious faiths differ. As it happens, I am a Catholic, and in my Celtic days, I was deeply involved in my commitment to the Celtic cause – so much so, that when we beat Rangers, I always wanted to rub it in. If I scored a goal against Rangers, I took a great delight in running behind their goal and making my feelings clear to their supporters. And even today, when I watch Celtic and Rangers trying to give each other a hiding, there is still no way that I want the old enemy to win.

Derby games between Manchester United and Manchester City are somewhat different, although the players of each team are keen to score a success. Manchester United are a Catholic club, too – but, like Celtic, they have often fielded players of other religions. So far as I know, City don't care about a player's religion – so long as he does his stuff on the field. And I have no argument against that attitude, either.

I do think that if you are a Mancunian born and bred, you feel more deeply about one club or the other, just as I felt deeply about Celtic doing well, when we played Rangers. But in any event, these days both United and City have each got so many players who were not born locally that the old bitterness in the rivalry is missing, to a large degree.

How can I, for instance, feel bitter about the opposition when players such as Willie Donachie and Asa Hartford, both Scotland internationals, like myself – and friends of mine – are in the side? Yes, I play to win a derby game, for the sake of our supporters; but it doesn't mean I dislike my opponents.

And while I'm on a Scottish theme, let me answer a question which was put to me not long ago. It was simply this: 'Do you think Tommy Docherty (a Scot himself, remember) has gone for too many Scots at Old Trafford?' It's a fair question, because during The Doc's reign, United have had quite a Scottish clan – almost a team of Scots, in fact. There were Denis Law, Willie Morgan, Jim McCalliog, and still there are Alex Forsyth, Martin Buchan, Stewart Houston, Jim Holton and myself. But I don't believe Tommy Docherty leans too much towards Scottish talent – apart from the fact that he has simply gone for players who, he felt, would fit into the United style, I can't resist adding that we can all play a bit!

9 There Must Be Laughs Along The Way

If Soccer is big business, and results are important, it's also essential to remember that there must be some laughs along the way. I've had my share of the fun, aided and abetted by people who can take a joke when it's directed against themselves. Manager Tommy Docherty has slipped a chapter of his own into this book – yes, I've had a peek at it, boss – and he told you the tale of the Press lads' gear which went missing in Denmark. There's a punch-line to the story, because after they had got their belongings back, I sneaked into their room the night before we were due to fly back home . . . and I removed the lot again.

The two Press lads – yes, they're still good pals of mine – had decided to have a final night out, and I figured it would be in the small hours when they returned. Sure enough, when they did get back, they just wanted to get straight to their beds . . . and that was where I found them, when I went in next morning, ostensibly to give them an early call. I reminded them that we were due to leave shortly, so they'd better get cracking and pack their bags. When they discovered there were no bags, and nothing to put into them any way, they were almost in tears. And I nearly choked with silent laughter, as each started to accuse the other of having been the culprit this time.

I slipped quietly away, and – with only a few minutes to go before departure time – returned and dumped all their belongings in their laps. Frantically, they began packing, and I left them to it. Just as the coach was ready to leave for the airport, they arrived, puffing and panting, and climbed aboard. And as people yelled out questions such as 'Where have you two been?' and 'What's been keeping you?', one of them grinned and came up with an answer which brought a roar of laughter. Standing at the front of the coach, and burdened with all his hurriedly-retrieved luggage, he countered smartly: 'We're only here for the gear!'

It was during that trip to Denmark that another howler was perpetrated – this time absolutely unintentionally. We paid a flying visit to one of the islands for a game, and some of the Pressmen stayed behind with our manager, to do some feature material. I promised that I would give them a ring after the game to let them know the result. Unfortunately, during the first half of the match, I found myself taking quite a bit of stick from a big, strong Danish defender, and in the end I retaliated . . . and received marching orders. At the end of the match, I put a call through to United's hotel, and told the Pressmen: 'We won, 3-2 – and I got sent off.'

Now, a year previously, exactly the same thing had happened during a game in Spain . . . and there was no way I could convince the guys I was calling that I wasn't up to another of my tricks. They simply wouldn't believe that I had received marching orders – I think they were even a bit sceptical about the 3-2 result. Two hours later, when we had flown back and reached our hotel, I found the newspapermen still convinced that I'd been making up the sending-off incident – and, to be on the safe side, they hadn't sent the story back to England.

There's always plenty of fun, when the Scotland international team gets together, and although I have already told you that I neither drink nor smoke, I think you would have a hard time convincing Scotland team-manager Willie Ormond (himself a teetotaller) of the truth of that statement – at least, the first part of it. For he still has vivid memories of an early-morning incident in which he thought he had caught a burglar . . . and discovered it was yours truly.

We were attending an international get-together in Scotland, and this particular evening Willie Ormond had given us permission to go out for a few hours, so a few of us wandered down town, and there we sat in an hotel, talking football, as usual, and relaxing quite happily. One of the lads suggested that we phone Willie Ormond at the team's headquarters and ask if we could return a bit later than planned, and when we did so, the manager gave us the go-ahead. We were back pretty well on schedule, but then we found there was just one snag – when we reached our hotel, which stopped serving at 10pm, everything was locked up.

We stood outside, pondering on the best course of action, and as we were discussing the matter, one of the lads noticed that a third-floor room had a window open. That was the side where the Scotland players were accommodated, so we had no doubts in our minds that the room belonged to one of our party, and that if it was occupied, one of our team-mates would be sleeping the sleep of the just. So there was no danger of causing a disturbance if one of us shinned up the drainpipe to the room, let himself in that way, then went down to unlock the front door for the rest of the lads. All that remained was to decide which of us should go up the drainpipe . . . and I was voted the man for the job.

I agreed to give it a go, and there was no problem as I scaled the drainpipe and reached the open window. Then I quietly let myself into the room, and – just in case one of my team-mates was fast asleep – I began to tip-toe towards the door. It was pretty dark, but I could just make out which direction to take, and I had got half-way across the room when, suddenly, a figure sat bolt upright in bed. I don't know which of us was the more taken aback, but when the figure sharply inquired 'Who's that?' I was certain about one thing. It wasn't a team-mate . . . it was Willie Ormond.

So what do you say when you're sneaking past the manager's bed, shortly after midnight? – I thought quickly, then managed to smile – though he couldn't see that – and tried to assume as nonchalant an appearance as possible, as I headed for the door and said quietly: 'See you in the morning.' And then I was gone. I can tell you I moved pretty quickly down the stairs, though, and within seconds I had let the lads in through the front door and we were all away to our rooms. The next morning, nothing was said, but I knew I'd been tabbed. One of Willie Ormond's favourite expressions is 'You're some man, you.' And more than once, the following day, he would give me a penetrating stare, shake his head, then murmur: 'You're some man, you . . .' Even today, I doubt if I could persuade the Scotland team manager that all I'd had to drink that evening, while I was out, was . . . Coke.

Incidentally, although two players usually room together, when a team is away from home, I'm an exception to the rule, because I like a room to myself. It's not that I'm anti-social, or object to hearing another guy snore; it's simply that I'm a restless creature, and I want to be able to get up when it suits me in a morning, without having to disturb someone else who may be wanting a lie-in.

The hotel where we stayed in Scotland has one little room which, on this occasion, had been allocated to Archie Gemmill. Like myself, Archie is no giant, and he was snugly tucked up in bed one night when the door opened, and there stood a bunch of his team-mates – armed with chicken legs. Well, you couldn't swing a cat round in that little single room, so there was nowhere for Archie to go, when the bombardment began. He did his best to protect himself by ducking under the bedclothes, as chicken legs rained around his head . . . then we left him to enjoy his 'supper.'

Yes, there are still plenty of laughs, even if professional football is a very serious business, and you have to learn to take a joke, as well as be able to share in the fun. You can always tell when things are right, at club or international level, by the laughter – or lack of it – when the players are together in the dressing-room. If the lads are cracking jokes and ribbing each other, then the team spirit is buoyant. And in every team there are one or two players who are also the comedians – even though they may not realise this themselves.

Sometimes something which starts out as a bit of a joke becomes a serious matter – I'm thinking now, for instance, of the time goalkeeper Alex Stepney became Manchester United's official penalty taker. The team spirit at Old Trafford then was good enough, but it wasn't a time for taking our football lightly, for we had been struggling for First Division survival. Many a goalkeeper has expressed an ambition to play at centre-forward in a match, but off-hand, I cannot remember any goalkeeper becoming his team's recognised spot-kick expert, even for a brief spell. Alex enjoys having a crack at goal from the penalty spot, and it was during a pre-season training session that the question cropped up.

Someone, obviously, has to be the penalty taker of the team, but at that time, no one in United's side was keen to tackle the job. I think we'd all lost confidence. As it turned out, during the training session, when the emphasis was on taking penalties, Alex proved to be the most successful marksman of the lot – and, when it became clear that there was a shortage of volunteers, Alex just grinned and said: 'I'll take the penalties.' We took it as a joke – until Tommy Docherty said: 'All right – if you want to, you can have a go.' And for a spell, Alex became Manchester United's spot-kick man, as well as the goalkeeper. Nowadays, of course, Gerry Daly is very much the penalty expert.

Which reminds me that if there's a wrong way of doing things – other than taking penalties – Gerry is the man who will do it. In a way, he's what you might call an unconscious comedian . . . and, as he's Irish himself, he might just appreciate that expression. With Stewart Houston and myself, Gerry is one of the team's talkers on the field – and he's got plenty to say for himself off it. He's also something of a contradiction, one of the exceptions to the rule that professional footballers must watch their diet, especially just before a game. Gerry smokes, he takes the odd drink, he likes staying up to watch the late-night movie; and he's always ready to challenge anyone, no matter what game is involved. Sometimes he's never even heard of the game, but that doesn't stop him believing he will beat his opponent at it.

Most of all, though, the lads rib him about the food he eats. Gerry lives on a basic diet of chips. He has to have them with everything. Even before a game, he still wants chips . . . washed down with a soft drink. And in a restaurant, you don't need to ask Gerry what he's having; you could place the order for him . . . steak and chips, or scampi and chips.

Yet despite his addiction to fried potatoes, Gerry seems to take no harm. Other players might put on weight, but he remains as lean as a beanpole. And he still has limitless stamina. I don't think Gerry worries about a single thing, and I reckon the same goes for Alex Forsyth. He may be a fellow-Scot, but you can believe me when I say that people like myself, Martin Buchan and Jim Holton find it extremely difficult to understand a word Alex says. So what chance have the English lads in the side? Everyone tries to imitate the way Alex talks, but only he can produce the authentic, almost unintelligible accent. Because he's the genuine original.

Naturally, when Manchester United were going to Wembley, we were all on at Alex about his accent, and warning him that he would have to speak clearly, to make himself understood, when he walked up the steps to the royal box. And we wanted to know what he intended to say to the Queen. 'Och,' he answered, 'I know all right what I'm going to say . . . I'm going to have a word with her about the income-tax I'm paying!'

When it comes to preparing for a game, Alex seems to anoint himself with just about every potion known to man. Vaseline, oil, Vick up his nose, sticky plasters round his shinguards, the lot. Sometimes we kid him that he's afraid of catching cold when he's out on the park; at other times, if the weather is warm, we suggest that he's using lotion to make sure he gets a suntan.

Home or away, the players of Manchester United usually find something to give them a laugh, and Martin Buchan came in for some kidding when we toured Australia a couple of years or so ago. Martin is a man who minds his own business and does his own thing – and during that tour, he literally vanished from sight for a long time, on one occasion.

When he finally reappeared, and was asked what had taken him so long, he said matter-of-factly that he'd hired a car and gone off to see an uncle. Fair enough . . . but we were startled to learn that the uncle lived 400 miles away. I know Australia's a big country, but that's still a long way to go for a social visit. Sometimes I think that Martin sits down to figure out what no one else will be likely to do – then decides that's what he'll do. Still, I suppose it's a good job we're not all cast in the same mould; which is why Stuart Pearson, and not myself, wears the No.9 jersey for Manchester United.

I'm being serious now, when I say that I think Stuart has the hardest job in the side, if for no other reason than that he wears the No.9 shirt. I'm not superstitious, as I have said, but when I joined United, I was told that the No.9 jersey would be mine. Politely, but firmly, I replied that I would rather wear another jersey, and I imagine that Tommy

Docherty must have thought I was some kind of a crackpot.

My reasoning was simple enough, though: if you wear No.8 or No.10, people – and I include opponents – tend to regard you as an inside-right or an inside-left, a player more likely to operate in a midfield role than as a striker. So it's easier to let them think this – and you have a better chance of getting into the scoring act. If you go out with a No.9 on your back, you are immediately tagged as the centre-forward, the man whose out-and-out mission is to stick the ball in the net. And you're a marked man from the start. That's why I reckon Stuart is playing in the most difficult position in United's side; he's the man they all expect to see scoring two or three goals, every time out. Fortunately, he is exceptionally gifted as a footballer, as I have pointed out before. I just hope that if he reads this, he won't be wanting to swap shirts with me!

Mention goals to a striker, and he'll tell you that every one he scores is a good 'un, no matter whether it comes by design or accident. The funniest goal I ever scored was during a European Cup-tie, when Celtic played League of Ireland club Waterford, at Lansdowne-road, Dublin. I was all of twenty-five yards out when a hard-hit pass reached me, and the only thing I could do was back-heel the ball in the hope that a team-mate would get it. Imagine my astonishment – and the disgust of the Waterford defenders – when that back-heel sped hard and low, and finished in the back of the net. It was some introduction to European Cup football for me, all right.

Dublin is a long way from Dallas, in Texas, but when Manchester United toured the US in the summer of 1976, we were the ones who got a real surprise. We were due to play Dallas Tornado, and the Americans made the game a real production number. Before the start, each member of the Tornado side made his entrance on to the pitch astride a horse. Each player was wearing a cowboy outfit too, and as some of the guys were men from English League clubs, it won't surprise you when I say that they looked distinctly uneasy on their gee-gees. Bobby Hope, from West Brom, was introduced as Bobby 'Paleface' Hope; and former Manchester United man Jimmy Ryan, who went to Luton, was Jimmy 'Quickdraw' Ryan. Moments before the game was scheduled to begin, two men drove a stagecoach on the pitch, and as the coach careered around, players scrambled out of the way and fled in all directions.

That didn't end the entertainment, for at half-time, an aircraft appeared overhead . . . and from 7,000 feet, a guy parachuted down into the centre circle. Then there was some gimmick concerning the late Howard Hughes' will, and the parachutist called out a number. The person whose programme corresponded to that number clicked for a holiday in Hawaii.

When we played in Chicago, the fans were entertained by pop groups at half-time, and when the final whistle had blown, 2,000 fireworks went up in the air. I use the word fireworks loosely, because from the crescendo of sound, you could have been forgiven for thinking that the Americans had launched a giant spaceship. Those fireworks really were like big rockets. By contrast, Vancouver was very much like England – there was no razzmataz. Just imagine, though, if we kicked off the season at Old Trafford wearing stetsons and riding bucking broncos!

I haven't always found tangling with referees a laughing matter, but there was one occasion when the man in the middle and I were able to grin at each other and call it quits. We had played at St Andrew's, and the referee that day had awarded Birmingham a penalty which, in my view, was never on. The following season, we went to Villa Park, and when I saw that we had got the same referee again, I thought 'Here goes . . .' As the game progressed, I found myself disagreeing more and more with his decisions, and in the end, I told him straight: 'You're having a stinker today.' He didn't bother to argue with me, but he got his own back a couple of minutes later, when I ballooned the ball over the bar from just a few yards, and thus missed the gift chance of an equaliser. Quick as a flash, the ref was alongside to counter: 'I'm not having half the stinker that you are!'

It wasn't long before I decided that Jack Taylor was the best referee in English football; and Gordon Hill was a guy who could give as good as he got, when it came to the verbal patter. This is one of the problems for players, because one week you get a ref who will swap the repartee, and the next you'll get one who won't stand for a word out of place. So you feel you never quite know where you are.

I like to think that so far as Clive Thomas is concerned, I played a part in helping him to be one of the best referees in the game – even if it didn't seem like there was going to be a happy ending, at the time. It was a derby game against Manchester City at Maine-road, and Mike Doyle, the City defender, and I had tangled a few times. Then came an incident which produced the flashpoint. I knew it was going to be a foul by Mike on myself, and as I picked myself up, I got the ball and threw it at him. Clive Thomas issued marching orders to the pair of us.

Frankly, I felt that if we walked, there could be repercussions from the crowd, and I said so to Clive. 'Look, we've shaken hands . . . now let's get on with the game,' I argued. But Clive, who would be the first to admit that in those days he was 'notebook-happy', was adamant. Mike Doyle and I had to take an early bath. Still I persisted in arguing that the best thing to do was get on with the game; so Clive Thomas took both TEAMS off the field. And during this cooling-down period, he made it plain once more that there was no way Mike Doyle and myself – by now, the best of friends again – were going to take part in the rest of the match. In the end, Clive made and won his point.

Mike and I appeared before a disciplinary committee, and it was two weeks' suspension and a £100 fine. But there was so much controversy, and the proceedings were so long drawn-out that by the time Mike and I were serving our 'sentences', I think everyone had had just about enough. Including Clive Thomas. For it's my sincere belief that the Maine-road incident was the one which persuaded him it was time to take a more tolerant approach, to leave the notebook in his pocket and see what the quiet word would do. And I'm sure he would confirm that he's a better referee these days than ever before. He can be the man in the middle for me any time.

Having had my say about referees – one or two of them, anyway – let me air my views on crowds, players and clubs. The crowds first: and so far as Burnley and Everton fans go, I don't think Manchester United win the popularity stakes. Not that anyone outside Old Trafford's faithful wants us to sweep all before us; but the folk who support the teams at Turf Moor and Goodison Park seem to take a special delight in seeing their sides trying to put one across us. I like playing at Anfield, though, because the Liverpool fans are able to invest their remarks with humour, even when they're giving you some stick. And believe it or not, I have actually heard our own supporters being outshouted on our own Old Trafford ground. No, it wasn't when the Kop came over from Anfield . . . it was during our Second Division days, when Sunderland were the visitors, and the Geordies were down from Wearside. I'll say this for the Burnley supporters, too – they may not like us overmuch, and they may be a bit thin on the ground, even at Turf Moor . . . but when they come to Old Trafford, they certainly make themselves heard. And I've no complaints about that.

The two clubs who epitomise what the game is all about – and that's winning – are Leeds and Liverpool. I've been known to knock Leeds, and I'll admit that Liverpool's style isn't United's. Yet whenever I've been with players from Elland-road and Anfield, during the Scotland international get-togethers, I've been impressed by their attitude. At times, it's seemed that Scotland WERE Leeds and Liverpool, and the players from both these clubs show what football means to them, in training as well as when the action is for real. I can see how it is that Leeds and Liverpool have stayed at the top for a decade and more – players such as Billy Bremner, for instance, seem to think a five-a-side two days before a big game is as important as the match itself.

The wee man from Leeds once referred to me as 'the poison dwarf' – he seemed to be half-joking, half-serious at the time, and while I didn't go too deeply into it, I got the impression that I'd earned this description from the way I went into five-a-side matches. No punches pulled, and ready to give as good as I got. From what I've said about the players at Leeds, you can take it that I didn't mind Billy applying this descriptive phrase to me . . . if anything, I considered it a compliment from one real professional to another.

Where football is concerned, superlatives become commonplace, and players who are not always out of the top drawer often command glowing adjectives. So far as I'm concerned, there are only a couple of footballers who truly deserve the title of superstar – and they're both on the Continent. One is Franz Beckenbauer, the other is Johan Cruyff. And if I had to choose, Beckenbauer would be my No.1 every time. Yet that doesn't mean to say there are no great players in English football.

Who does excite me? – Kevin Keegan. Take him out of the England team, I reckon, and they would lose a lot of their lustre. Sure, England would still win matches, but in Keegan they have that extra-special spark, the player who can produce something different. I think Liverpool have another player who could become an idol . . . David Fairclough, the red-haired youngster who burst upon the First Division scene and played such a dazzling part in Liverpool's run through to the championship and UEFA Cup. He's tall, somewhat gangling in appearance – but how he can 'skin' defenders. AND he packs a shot.

Another player who, I hope, will live up to the image I have of him is Tony Currie. When I played against him in his days with Sheffield United, I found it was almost impossible to take the ball from him. He is a gifted player, able to weigh up situations, spray accurate passes, and score a goal or two. But to be frank, I think that he had stayed long enough at Bramhall-lane. It's difficult, if not impossible, to be the inspiration of your side every week. Now that he's at Leeds, and in a team which is studded with internationals, I believe he will convince everyone of his genuine ability to be a top-class player who can entertain, excite – and help to produce results.

You'll notice that I've been talking just about forwards. And I have to say that it's forwards – attackers – who delight and excite me. Defenders don't do anything for me, although I acknowledge that they are essential, and that there are some extremely good ones around. I suppose that if you asked a defender to talk about the players he admires, you'll find he tends to think of other defenders, and to extol their qualities as back-four men.

My final choice of a player who really rates may seem surprising. I'll confess that he doesn't excite me in the same way that Keegan, Currie and Fairclough do, because he's not that type of player. He's a steady, hard-working footballer who does his job supremely well. In short, he's an honest-to-goodness professional. And his name is Alan Gowling. Once upon a time, he played for Manchester United; then he moved to Huddersfield Town, and found himself going down the divisions. When he moved to Newcastle United, he finally hit the jackpot. He may seem to have an awkward running style, but there's nothing clumsy about the way he tucks away the scoring chances. And don't forget that his goals come without the aid of penalties.

I'm not saying that he would have been as great a hit if he had remained at Old Trafford, and I'm not saying, either, that Manchester United were wrong to sell him. What I am saying, and what cannot be disputed, is that since he went to Newcastle, he found the right niche for himself, and he maintained a consistent record of sticking the ball into the back of the net. And when you can compete on equal terms with someone like 'Supermac', you must have something about you.

While I'm at it, I'll tell you something else. I've discovered since I came down south that you need more than skill, to be a success in English League football. You need real will to win, sheer determination, and a refusal to accept that you're second-best. Believe me, EVERYONE you come up against in the First Division is really trying . . . and that, of course, means you have to try that bit harder yourself to come out on top. I think we've got one or two young players at Old Trafford who can make their mark.

As I have said previously, there is plenty of talent at Manchester United, and I've gone through a long list of names. Some of them are already established first-teamers, some are still youngsters, and some are on the fringe, as it were, having tasted top-class football, but still waiting to win a regular place. And the two I'm thinking of in particular are David McCreery and Arthur Albiston. Believe me, in the next season or two, everyone is going to realise that they're good players. As Willie Ormond might say to each of them : 'You're some man, you . . .'

So now we're back to Manchester United, and the more serious side of Soccer. We've ploughed a pretty hard road during the past few seasons, but the compensating factor for all of us is that we've faced the problems as they have arisen, and we've overcome them. As Tommy Docherty stressed, when I first joined, the only direction for Manchester United is upwards. Which is my cue to turn the spotlight on our promotion campaign . . .

10   Going Up...That's United

I must confess that I didn't exactly look forward to visiting
some of the Second Division outposts of Soccer. I had played
before big crowds for Celtic and Scotland, and I had got a
kick out of playing in front of the Old Trafford multitude,
and at grounds such as Anfield, Elland-road, St James's Park
and White Hart-lane. Then Manchester United were relegated and, suddenly, all that was at an end. Instead it meant
trips to places I had scarcely heard of – Eastville, Ashton
Gate, Bootham-crescent, The Den, the Manor Ground and
Brisbane-road.

Brisbane-road, in fact, was Manchester United's first stop
on their safari in the Second Division. The home of Orient,
who had gone so close themselves to exchanging places
with us in Division One, at the end of the 1973-74 season.
As United, Norwich and Southampton had gone down,
Middlesbrough, Luton and Carlisle had moved up – and
Orient had suffered as great a sickener as ourselves, for they
had been pipped at the post, as Carlisle edged into the third
promotion spot by a solitary point.

I could have a sort of academic sympathy for the London
club; but playing on their ground in front of 17,000 people
wasn't exactly my idea of all the thrills that Soccer could
offer. I had had my share of playing against the minnows,
too, in my days with Celtic, and when I joined Manchester
United, I wasn't anticipating trips to places with outlandish
and unfashionable names. And in saying that, I intend no
disrespect to Orient or their ground, or to any of the others
whom we encountered during that year when United were

sentenced to a term in the Second Division.

Looking back, indeed, I feel that perhaps it was a part of my Soccer education – and, for that matter, a part of Manchester United's, as well. Lots of people, I know, were secretly smug when United fell from First Division grace. They felt that no club had a divine right to be in the top flight, and they felt, too, that it would do United a bit of good to go 'slumming it' for a spell. United would learn just how the other half lived. Fair enough. But as it turned out, there was another side to the coin, for we all began to appreciate exactly the extent of the following Manchester United had, not just at Old Trafford, but right around the country. And the Second Division clubs, without exception, certainly had good cause to welcome our arrival, for wherever we played, the gates soared.

Figures like these tell the story . . . 22,500 at Cardiff, almost 24,000 at West Brom, 25,000 at Norwich, 26,000 at Fulham, 22,000 at Blackpool, 28,000 at Bristol City, 23,000 at Hull, 35,000 at Sheffield Wednesday, 26,000 at Oldham, almost 46,000 at Sunderland, 39,000 at Aston Villa, almost 38,000 at Bolton, nearly 22,000 at Nottingham Forest and Southampton. Not as many perhaps, as at Anfield or Old Trafford – but some of the clubs we played had their gates doubled or even trebled, when we were the visitors.

In part, this was due to the fact that many of our home-based supporters travelled around the country to see us playing for a place in the First Division again. In part, it was because we had supporters' branches all over the country. And in part, it was because of the tremendous crowd appeal the name of Manchester United had. At some grounds, they made the match against us all-ticket; and at every ground, they rubbed their hands in expectation of a big cash boost at the gate, when we were due.

As for Old Trafford, we found that our supporters had stuck with us. Almost 42,000 people turned up for the game against Millwall; 40,000-plus for games against Nottingham

Forest and Bristol Rovers; 46,500 for the Notts County match; 48,724 for the visit of Southampton; 41,500 for Oxford; 55,615 for Aston Villa; 60,585 for Sunderland; 41,200 for Orient; 51,000 for West Brom; 45,662 for Sheffield Wednesday; 47,000 for Bristol City; almost 45,000 for Hull City; 43,601 for Cardiff City; 56,000 for Norwich City; nearly 47,000 for York City; close on 53,000 for the visit of Fulham.

Gates such as these were phenomenal for the Second Division, and I honestly believe that no other club in the country, with the possible exception of Liverpool, could have come anywhere near to equalling figures like that. What would have been the effect, had we become just another mid-table team in Division two, it is difficult to say; but I still feel we would have averaged more than 35,000 at Old Trafford, and wooed more fans than usual to the other grounds on which we played. The matter was never put to the test, though, because we set off on the promotion chase like a house on fire, and left no doubt in anyone's mind that we were haring straight back to the First Division.

When it had become obvious that Manchester United were in very real danger of losing their place in the First Division, Sir Matt Busby had turned to Tommy Docherty and said: 'All right, if we're going to go down, let's go down in style.' What he meant was that United had made their name as an entertaining, attacking side, and that we should not leave memories behind us of a dour, unimaginative team intent only on keeping the opposition at bay. In the closing stages of our campaign against relegation, we began to go out with the idea in our minds that if we were to sink, then we would go down with all guns firing. And that was the mood in which we approached our battle to scale the Second Division obstacles and regain the top flight.

Two goals in the opening game at Orient gave us a flying start, and a 4-0 thrashing of Millwall at Old Trafford really set us alight. In that game, Gerry Daly slotted home a hat-trick, including two goals from the penalty spot, and began to earn himself a name as the penalty king. He's tucked away quite a few more since that match.

Fulham and Norwich led the way, with five points from three games apiece, while United had maximum points from their two matches. After four games, we hit the top – the only team in the Second Division to have won every game – and it was penalty-ace Daly again who popped up to score our winner in the match at Cardiff. We dropped our first point in our fifth game, when we drew 2-2 at Old Trafford against Nottingham Forest – Sammy McIlroy snatched our equaliser with 10 minutes to go – but we still led the field, for we were a point ahead of Norwich, who had played a game more, and two in front of Aston Villa, Fulham, Oxford, Blackpool and Notts. County. We drew at West Brom, beat Bristol Rovers 2-0, and did not lose until our 10th match of the season. This was at Carrow-road, and Norwich stuck two goals past us – ironically, the scorer each time was Ted MacDougall, late of United.

But we were still leading the pack, with 16 points from our 10 matches, which put us three ahead of Norwich, four ahead of Blackpool, and five in front of Sunderland, Fulham and York. We won at Fulham and Blackpool, beat Notts. County, Southampton and Oxford at Old Trafford, with Stuart Pearson claiming a hat-trick against United, and we had totalled 27 points from 16 matches. Norwich lagged five points behind us, Sunderland were eight points adrift, like Aston Villa . . . yes, we were racing away in the promotion stakes, and doing it in style.

Bristol City beat us at Ashton Gate, then we defeated Aston Villa 2-1 at Old Trafford, with two more goals from Gerry Daly . . . yes, one was a penalty. Hull beat us at Boothferry Park, but we got the better of Sunderland in a five-goal battle at Old Trafford, then shared in a fantastic eight-goal thriller against Sheffield Wednesday at Hillsborough. Goals? – It seemed impossible for either side to stop the flow, and the 35,000 fans were buzzing with excitement.

Stewart Houston started the scoring spree, after only seven minutes' play; then Sunley, Harvey and Shaw rocked us back on our heels, by delivering a three-goal salvo which made the spectators think we were going to be hammered. But straight after half-time, I got into the scoring act, then Stuart Pearson made it 3-3. Wednesday came at us again, and Sunley, scorer of their first goal, tucked away their fourth.

Still we were not beaten, and with nine minutes of the game remaining, Sammy McIlroy popped in the final goal, which made the scoreline 4-4, and ensured that we took a point. We had reached the half-way mark of our promotion campaign, and were still the pacemakers, with 32 points from 21 matches – five ahead of Sunderland, six in front of Norwich, although each of these clubs had a match in hand on ourselves. But we were showing that we could maintain the breakneck pace, and stay ahead.

The 22nd game meant that the opposition was the same as in our first match – Orient – but this time, at Old Trafford, we didn't score two goals without reply; instead, we had to be satisfied with a 0-0 draw, and our lead over Sunderland was cut to three points. But a win at York and at Old Trafford against West Brom – another Daly penalty – restored our five-point lead, although Sunderland narrowed the gap by a point when we lost at Oldham in the final League match of 1974. We then had 37 points from 25 games, were unbeaten at home, having won 10 and drawn two of the dozen matches played at Old Trafford . . . and we had won no fewer than six of our 13 away games.

The FA Cup occupied our attention, when we were drawn at home against Walsall, in the third round, and a 0-0 scoreline meant we had to travel to the Midlands for a replay. Walsall got the better of us, but as they also knocked out First Division Newcastle United in the fourth round, we felt that our defeat had been no disgrace – and, of course, we could say, as we had said the previous season, that now we could concentrate on the League. Except that on this occasion, our sights were on the top of the ladder, instead of us being concerned about the trap-door beneath our feet.

Two Jim McCalliog goals sank his old club, Sheffield Wednesday, at Old Trafford, then we drew 0-0 at Roker Park. So Sunderland and Norwich had each played 27 matches, like United, and we had a five-point lead on Bob Stokoe's team and were nine points ahead of Norwich, while 10 points separated us from fourth-placed Aston Villa and the fifth club, West Brom, although they each had a game in hand on us.

But matches in hand still had to be won . . . and we had the points in the bag. Still, we got a bit of a shock when, instead of adding to our 40-point tally, we stayed on the same mark after a home match against Bristol City, for these promotion outsiders scored the only goal of the game at Old Trafford – just one minute from time. But a few people immediately started to ask: 'Are United about to slip?'

Sunderland had lost 3-2 at Blackpool, so our Lancashire neighbours had done us a good turn there, but Norwich had won at Bristol Rovers, and Aston Villa had scored a 3-1 victory at Notts. County. West Brom, on the other hand, had slipped down to seventh in the table, after having been beaten 3-0 by Southampton at The Hawthorns.

When Oxford United defeated us at their Manor Ground and Sunderland beat Cardiff at Roker Park, the points gap at the top was narrowed to three, but in mid-February we regained our winning touch with a 2-0 win over Hull City at Old Trafford, and moved on to 42 points, four ahead of Sunderland. Then, however, we went to Villa Park and failed to score, while our opponents put two goals past us –

but Fulham did us a good turn, by inflicting a first home defeat on Sunderland, although Norwich, with a single-goal win at Carrow-road against Oldham, edged on to 38 points, like the Roker club. There were 11 matches now standing between Manchester United and promotion.

With 10 games to go, we had moved on to 44 points, still four clear of Sunderland, and six ahead of third-placed Norwich. We scored a convincing 4-0 home victory over Cardiff City, and I had the satisfaction of sticking away our final goal, one minute after Sammy McIlroy had scored. Two minutes later, the referee had blown for time. But we faced a tough one in our next assignment, for we were away to Bolton Wanderers, and while they were not making any real bid to get into the fight for a top-three place, they had a useful record and were in eighth place in the table. United fans flocked to that game, of course, and Burnden Park had one of its best gates for years – almost 38,000. For United, the 29th minute was the best of the match, because that was when Stuart Pearson put the ball in the Bolton net . . . and that was how the scoreline stayed, to the end of the match.

Nine games to go, 46 points in the bag . . . five ahead of Sunderland, six ahead of Villa, seven in front of Norwich. We were all a bit relieved to come away from Bolton with a win, but we now began to get the feeling that nothing was going to go wrong on the final, all-important lap of the promotion race. And it didn't, although in our next game, Ted MacDougall scored his usual goal against his old club, and Norwich took a point from us at Old Trafford.

But we went to Nottingham, and Gerry Daly got the only goal of the game against Forest – not a penalty, this time – and then I scored the winner when we beat York 2-1 at Old Trafford, to take United to 52 points from 37 matches and increase our lead over second-placed Sunderland to seven points. I scored the only goal of the game at Southampton, while Sunderland were beating Hull at Roker

E

Park, and Gerry Daly was our marksman against Fulham at Old Trafford, while Sunderland were losing at Oxford.

By then, we had only two games to go, and had an eight-point lead over Aston Villa, who had slipped into second place, leaving Sunderland and Norwich fighting to claim the third promotion spot. As the League table showed, we were home and dry, and we could afford to watch the other teams scrapping it out for the privilege of accompanying us into the First Division.

But we still wanted to assert our superiority over all our rivals, by going up as Second Division champions – doing it, as Sir Matt Busby had mentioned in a different connection a year previously, in style. And we achieved our objective, with a 2-2 draw in our final away match, against Notts. County, and a 4-0 victory over Blackpool at Old Trafford. Stuart Pearson scored twice, I got the third goal, and Brian Greenhoff tucked away the last one.

Our supporters – almost 59,000 of them – went delirious with delight, as the game against Blackpool ended, and Old Trafford was a sea of waving scarves and banners, a cauldron of sound as the fans roared their salute to Manchester United. We were back where we felt we belonged – in the First Division. Sadly for Sunderland, they found that they were doomed to yet another season in Division 2, after having stayed so closely on our heels right through the season. Now, of course, they are in the top flight, too.

But at the time, it really must have seemed like the bitter end for them, because their hopes flickered and faded as the various teams made their final push. We had collected 61 points from our 42 matches; Sunderland, having played their total number of games, and finished with 51 points, saw Aston Villa five points ahead and Norwich two points ahead, and each club still had a game to go. It was a sickener for Bob Stokoe and his men, and I knew exactly how they must be feeling, for their final game at Villa Park had been the last of their slender hopes.

Unfortunately for them, while we were giving Blackpool that four-goal hiding, Villa were showing scant sympathy for Bob Stokoe and his players, as they scored twice in the last 11 minutes to destroy any ideas Sunderland might have had of snatching third place . . . and Norwich completed the Roker club's downfall, as they tore into Portsmouth and whacked three goals past them at Fratton Park.

Meanwhile, down at the foot of the First Division, Luton, Chelsea, Tottenham and Carlisle had been slogging it out, to see which of them could stave off relegation. In the end, Carlisle and Luton were doomed, and at the last gasp, Spurs secured safety and left Chelsea, Tommy Docherty's old club, sadly reflecting that they would accompany Luton and Carlisle through the trap-door.

Manchester United, however, had achieved their promotion ambitions in the grand manner. Crowds flocking to see us play, goals flowing – mostly from us – and a convincing campaign which had seen us lead the field from the early weeks of the season. We had lost only one of our 21 home matches – against Bristol City – and won 17 of them, scoring 45 goals and conceding only a dozen. Away from home, we had won nine matches and drawn half a dozen, and scored 21 goals while conceding 18.

We hadn't gone far in the FA Cup, and in the League Cup we had been knocked out when we had had visions of going all the way to Wembley. But if we were not going into Europe the following season, we were returning to the First Division; and that was the most important thing.

11 Chasing The Title

The moment of truth . . . that was how the critics saw the start of season 1975-76 for Manchester United. Runaway winners of the Second Division championship we might have been, but now United were being thrown in against the crack teams of the First Division, and this, it was said, would soon sort out the men from the boys. I must admit, too, that many of us at Old Trafford, including manager Tommy Docherty, wondered what sort of showing we would make, on our return to the arena which has often been called the toughest club competition in the world.

Just a year earlier, after we had kicked off our Second Division term by taking eight points from four matches, our manager had been saying that the Second Division need hold no fears for us . . . provided that we did not become over-confident. In fact, he also made two other points – that United could emerge a much stronger club for the experience, because young players would get the chance to find their feet and develop the skills which they would find difficult to produce in the First Division.

'This is particularly applicable to Manchester United, because we have a very young side by League standards, and two or three of the players joined English football comparatively late in their careers,' he summed up. Exactly one year later, when we had played our first five matches after our return to the First Division, Tommy Docherty was saying: 'It's great to see Manchester United at the top of the table . . .'

Once again, he added some timely words of warning,

as he pointed out that it was a long way to the end of the season and, therefore, too early to forecast that United would remain at the top. But he also made a promise that we would have 'a darned good try, and that our attempt will be with the style of football that has given us a good start to the season.'

The Doc summed up United's approach to the game with these words: 'An attacking game is the only one we know how to play, these days. I think that even if I wanted to change the tactics and get the team playing defensively, the lads wouldn't really know how. It isn't in their make-up now to be negative and cautious, and I am very happy about that, because it means we have a team instinctively wanting to be bold and adventurous.'

He believed that because of United's tradition as a foot-balling side, the club had automatically recruited players with the right outlook. 'An attacking policy may occa-sionally put us in trouble and lose us matches; but in the long run, it is the basis, I believe, for a healthy success. By healthy, I mean success that is good to watch.' So the keynote was attack – and entertain. And that suited me, for one, down to the ground. It also suited our legion of supporters, who had been bred on success achieved by teams of genuine flair.

Tommy Docherty stressed the need for United to play positive football. He talked about the team having the will to take a chance and go forward, and the gospel he preached was taken up enthusiastically by the players. Sure, we would defend when the need to defend arose; but as soon as we got possession of the ball, it was a case of pushing forward and trying to score goals. And there is no doubt that our way of carrying the game to the opposition – home and away – was refreshing, in most people's eyes.

One or two people had tried to take some of the gloss off our promotion success by pointing out that the op-position in the Second Division hadn't been all that hot;

by adding that we had been remarkably lucky in not finding ourselves bogged down on heavy grounds, during the worst of the winter months; and by concluding that we would be punished for our adventurous style of play, once we came up against the vastly experienced sides of the First Division. In short, while we might carry on for a while where we had left off in the Second Division, it wouldn't be long before we had run out of steam.

I could claim the honour of being the first United player to score, on our return to Division 1: for when we went to Molineux, I was on the mark twice late in the game, so that United kicked off with a 2-0 victory. 'A good start,' conceded the cynics. 'But let's see what happens when they tackle Birmingham at St. Andrew's in the next match.' What happened was that we scored two goals again, without reply.

And when Sheffield United visited Old Trafford, we had an audience of almost 56,000 people for our first match on home ground. They savoured every moment of that game, too, for we ran riot against the team which had only just missed claiming a place in Europe, the previous spring. Stuart Pearson scored twice, Gerry Daly and Sammy McIlroy got a goal apiece, and Len Badger put through his own goal. We won 5-1.

Coventry came to Old Trafford, and they played well enough to get a draw; in fact, they provided us with our sternest test to date. Then we went to Stoke, and had one or two narrow escapes before cashing in on our good luck by finishing as 1-0 winners, with the aid of an own goal from Alan Dodd.

On the day that Tommy Docherty was named the new season's first Manager of the Month – it was a personal 'hat-trick', because in our promotion season he had twice won this monthly award – we took on Tottenham Hotspur at Old Trafford, and more than 51,000 people eagerly anticipated another victory flourish from Manchester United.

It was a game I'll remember for two or three things. First, we went a goal down after only four minutes, when Chris Jones got the ball into the net; then there was a bomb scare, while the game was in progress; and thirdly, I could claim to have a foot in the goal which set us on the road to victory.

Everyone was concentrating on the game, and we were putting everything into the effort of trying to equalise, when a flashing light appeared on the roof of one of the touchline dug-outs. It had been put there by the police, presumably as a sort of signal to their men stationed around the ground. The next thing that happened, as play continued, was that a loudspeaker message told the crowd there had been a telephone call saying that half a dozen bombs were due to go off at 3.30 p.m., and the fans were asked to have a good look round and tell the police if they spotted any suspicious articles or objects on the terraces or in the stands.

Frankly, the impact of the announcement didn't really get through to the players on the pitch; we were all too busy playing a fast and furious game of football. And the fans didn't seem to be too worried by what they obviously considered to be a hoax call, for they continued to roar out encouragement to United. The minutes ticked away towards 3.30, and I'm told that as the final seconds drew close to the deadline, people did go quiet, as if waiting for the big explosion. But the deadline came and went, and nothing happened . . . except that Manchester United equalised. And that brought a crescendo of cheers which would surely have outdone any explosion caused by a bomb going off.

The scoring move started when I raced into space to take a pass from Jimmy Nicholl, and I took the ball on, then crossed it, knee-high; the ball was travelling at speed across the Spurs goalmouth, and the defenders got themselves into a bit of a tangle – so much so that Smith and Pratt went together to try to clear the danger, and all John

Pratt could do was steer the ball past 'keeper Pat Jennings. That was Manchester United's third goal in half a dozen matches which had been scored by courtesy of our opponents, and we weren't complaining.

You might call it good luck; but remember that own goals often come as a result of the pressure to which defenders are being subjected . . . so I think it is fair to say that it showed the extent of the attacking which United were doing, game by game. Just on half-time, Gerry Daly scored from the penalty spot, and he netted another goal a couple of minutes after the restart. Incidentally, Gerry – who had scored with nine spot-kicks the previous season – was converting the first one to be awarded to United this time out.

With 15 minutes to go, Spurs were awarded a penalty, but Jimmy Neighbour failed to profit from this chance, and although Martin Chivers struck a second goal for Tottenham eight minutes from time, it was too little and too late to affect the result. So we finished 3-2 ahead, and continued our bid to stay among the championship pacesetters.

In the Football League Cup, we were drawn against Brentford, and I'll admit that perhaps there was a shade of good fortune about our victory, for we ran out winners by the odd goal in three. Then we travelled to Loftus-road, to take on Queen's Park Rangers, who were lying fourth in the table, and in the first couple of minutes, we had a set-back, for David Webb put Rangers ahead. We lost Tommy Jackson with an ankle injury, after play had been going for about half an hour, and Tony Young came on as substitute.

With the game almost an hour old, Rangers were awarded a penalty, but Alex Stepney saved the spot-kick from Stan Bowles, so we were still in with a chance, but the game ended with the scoreline still reading 1-0 for Rangers. However, United still sat proudly astride the top of the First Division table, with seven games gone; we had taken 11 points out of 14, like West Ham (they were second, on goal average). Then came Rangers, who had moved up one, Coventry, Everton, Leeds, Liverpool and Derby County.

Fifty thousand people saw Stewart Houston's goal beat Ipswich at Old Trafford, but we lost 2-1 at Derby, and faced a tremendous task in our next match – against our greatest rivals, Manchester City, at Maine-road. Of course, memories were revived of that final First Division game at Old Trafford two seasons previously, and it was obvious that there would be a real atmosphere about this renewal of old rivalries.

More than 46,000 fans rolled up to Maine-road for the derby game, and half of them, at least, were rooting for Manchester City. It was a bit of a sickener when, with the match only 20 minutes old, young Jimmy Nicholl had the bad luck to put through his own goal and give City the lead – a case of that goal helping to cancel out one of those which had helped us win some of our previous matches. But we didn't allow that reverse to upset our rhythm, and on the half-hour we rattled in two goals in as many minutes. David McCreery scored the first, and I got the second. Two minutes later, Joe Royle equalised, and after 90 minutes, honours were still even.

A no-score home draw against Leicester, an exciting 2-1 victory over Aston Villa – away – in the next round of the League Cup, and that brought Manchester United to yet another challenging task . . . Leeds United at Elland-road. So far, we hadn't run out of ideas or steam, but everyone agreed that Leeds would test us all the way.

This was one of the games which would show how well we were equipped to stay the pace in the title race. Our draw against Leicester had taken us back to the top of the table, and Leeds' 2-1 win against Queen's Park Rangers the same afternoon had dislodged the London club from the leadership. Then came West Ham, Liverpool, Derby and Leeds, so we were in the thick of it all, and the way the leadership was see-sawing suggested that half a dozen clubs were going to be heavily involved in the title battle.

Rangers won, Liverpool and West Ham won, and Derby drew; and the only team in the top half-dozen to lose were . . . Leeds United. Sammy McIlroy did the damage, with two goals, and though Allan Clarke pulled one back, and Leeds never ceased to fight for the equaliser, we came out on top. More than that, we had played well enough to deserve our victory, as even our critics had to concede.

We defeated Arsenal 3-1 at Old Trafford, lost 2-1 at West Ham – I scored an equaliser, but Bobby Gould got the Hammers' winner – then took on Norwich on our own ground. The Canaries soaked up the pressure, and defended doggedly, and it looked as if time was running out for United; but with only 10 minutes of the game remaining, Stuart Pearson struck the goal that won the match for us. It was the second time we had had the ball in the net, for Tommy Jackson had 'scored' earlier in the second half, only to have the goal disallowed.

That victory saw us sitting on top of the table, with 21 points from the 15 matches we had played. West Ham were second on goal average, as they had been once before, and they had a match in hand; then came Queen's Park Rangers, on 20 points, Derby on 20, and Liverpool, who had played 14 games, on 19. Our next assignment was a trip to Anfield, on November 8, and we knew this would be one of our greatest tests of the season.

Some wag – obviously, a Liverpool fanatic – had daubed a slogan in paint on a slab of concrete by the motorway which led from Manchester to Merseyside, and it read: 'United will die on November 8.' Well, we didn't exactly die . . . but we did suffer a defeat, and I have to confess that we took quite a hammering, for most of the game.

Liverpool took only 12 minutes to streak into the lead, through Steve Heighway, and one minute after half-time, John Toshack made it two. Five minutes after that, we gained new hope, when Steve Coppell scored, but Kevin Keegan tucked away a third goal for Liverpool with 12 minutes to go, and that was that. We slipped down to fifth place in the League table, and West Ham became the new leaders, followed by Derby, Queen's Park Rangers and Liverpool. Was THIS where the Manchester United bubble began to burst?

An even bigger question mark was raised against our name, when we returned to Maine-road for a League Cup-tie and received a four-goal hiding. And in spite of us beating Aston Villa 2-0 at Old Trafford, the doubts were still evident as we lost 3-1 at Highbury, and scraped home 1-0 against Newcastle United on our own ground. It took Arsenal only 12 seconds to get their noses ahead; Alan Ball celebrated the removal of his name from the transfer list by claiming the quickest goal of the season, and only 10 minutes or so after that, United had Sammy McIlroy carried off on a stretcher, with a facial injury.

Next, Sammy Nelson sent over a centre which George Armstrong prodded goalwards . . . and Brian Greenhoff was unable to avoid sticking the ball into his own net. The own goals were not flowing all one way! Stuart Pearson put us back in the game, just inside the hour, but Armstrong scored a third goal for the Gunners, with one minute left for play.

That defeat, and our home victory over Newcastle, put Manchester United on the 25-point mark, after 19 matches, which meant that we were two points behind the leaders – by this time, Derby County – and lying in fourth position. The pace, the doubters felt, was beginning to tell on United. But we went to Ayresome Park and drew against Middlesbrough, and followed up with a victory – in another game away from home – against Sheffield United, whom we hammered 4-1.

Stuart Pearson struck our first goal to give us a flying start, with the game only three minutes old; Gordon Hill scored his first goal for United, and Stuart notched his second of the game, to give us a 3-1 lead. Four minutes from time, I was on the mark, and the final scoreline read 4-1. Nothing, it seemed, would go right for the Sheffield club, who had won only one of their 21 games, and were propping up the rest of the First Division.

We scored a home victory over the Wolves, with a last-minute winner from Gordon Hill, drew 1-1 when we visited Goodison Park, and I scored the winner in a three-goal game against Burnley at Old Trafford, so Manchester United reached the turn of the year with 33 points from 24 matches, and we lay second to Liverpool, with only goal average separating us from the Merseyside club.

In fact, only three points separated the top five clubs — behind us were Leeds, Derby County and Queen's Park Rangers — and it was becoming evident that the championship issue was going to remain an extremely tight affair, even though the challenge from West Ham seemed to be fading somewhat.

When Rangers came to Old Trafford and took a 10th-minute lead, it seemed that United might go down to defeat in a game which was worth four points to the winners. Ironically, it was a former United player, Don Givens, who had arrived at Loftus-road via Luton, who scored first for Rangers; but they surrendered their lead when Gordon Hill and Sammy McIlroy rapped back with goals. Another goal by Gordon took a point from Tottenham, and when we came up against Birmingham at Old Trafford, we were striving to ensure that we didn't lose an unbeaten home record which stretched back for exactly one year.

Birmingham were beginning to realise that they faced a battle against relegation, as they had done in previous seasons since their return to the First Division, and Alex Forsyth rammed in one of his specials, from 25 yards, to set United on the road to victory. Seven minutes later, and I was a marksman, but Birmingham still had something to fight for, when Peter Withe reduced the arrears after an hour's play. One minute from time, though, it was all over, when Sammy McIlroy struck.

By then, United had 38 points from 27 matches, and we were back in the driving seat, with Liverpool a point behind. But Leeds had come up to move menacingly into fourth place, just behind Derby, while Queen's Park Rangers, who were fifth and had 34 points, were still clearly in contention. One week later, and the leadership had changed hands again, for while Liverpool were beating Leeds 2-0 at Anfield, Manchester United were struggling to take a point from Coventry City at Highfield-road.

Les Cartwright came on as Coventry's substitute shortly after half an hour had gone, and only a minute after he had got into the action, he hammered home a 25-yard shot which flew past Alex Stepney and just inside the post – the wrong side of the post, of course, for United. We were fighting to complete a run of 10 matches without defeat, as well as to retain our leadership of the First Division and just as time appeared to be running out for us, I managed to snatch the goal which earned us a point.

It was the end of the first week in February, and the championship battle was still as tense and as tight as ever. Liverpool had 39 points from their 28 games, and we were second – on goal average. Derby, Leeds and Queen's Park Rangers were still going hard at it, too, and everyone who called himself a football fan was becoming excited at the prospect of a cliffhanger climax to the championship tussle, because the leadership was still swaying first one way, then the other, and not one of the clubs at the top appeared to be able to break clear of the pack. Rangers had climbed back into third place, Derby lay fourth, and Leeds were fifth. West Ham, in sixth spot, were seven points behind Liverpool and ourselves, so it looked a five-horse race.

Rangers edged to within a point of Liverpool and United, with a victory at White Hart-lane, then moved into second place by beating Ipswich, while we were on the losing end at Aston Villa, where we were defending a 14-match unbeaten run. That run came to an end, as Bobby McDonald slipped Villa into the lead, and although I scored my 14th goal of the season to equalise, Andy Gray, a fellow-Scot, who had cost Villa a £100,000 fee, settled the issue with a goal after play had been going just over an hour. We couldn't pull that one back and, in fact, at around the time Andy was getting that winner, I was leaving the field, limping out of the game and taking no further part in the action.

One hundred thousand people were at Wembley on Saturday, February 28, to see Manchester City take on Newcastle United in the final of the League Cup. So the attention of half the city of Manchester was concentrated on what was happening in London – where our rivals triumphed over the Magpies with a fine display of attacking football. But although everyone had a keen interest in the outcome of the League Cup final, they were also keeping one eye on what was happening in the various League matches around the country.

Liverpool were playing at Derby – and they returned home with a point; Queen's Park Rangers also took a point from Sheffield United, at Bramall-lane; Leeds United went to Coventry, and won; and Manchester United . . . well, we demolished West Ham completely at Old Trafford, with a 4-0 victory which brooked no argument at all. West Ham knew, then, that any lingering hopes they might have had of getting back into the championship fray had virtually ended; as for Manchester United, we were still very strongly in contention for the title . . . and now we were only 10 matches away from the finishing line.

People had been talking about Leeds going over the hill, but once again, as in past years, they were showing that they had not lost their fiercely competitive edge. As for Liverpool, it looked as if they might just have thrown away their chance of the championship when they lost 2-0 to Middlesbrough at Anfield, on the day that Derby were beating Newcastle and United were drawing with Wolves in the sixth round of the FA Cup. Now the talk was not just about the title . . . it was about the chances of the various contenders doing a double.

For ourselves and Derby, the title and the FA Cup were the targets; for Liverpool, it was the championship and the UEFA Cup. Rangers and Leeds were the two teams with no distractions – and with eight League games to go, Rangers were leading the way, with 45 points, two clear of Liverpool and Derby, who each had a match in hand, and two clear of Manchester United, who had two games in hand. Leeds were half a dozen points adrift, but they had three games in hand on Rangers, so they could yet put in a finishing burst, especially as they had to play at Old Trafford and at Loftus-road. Our next home engagement, in fact, was against Leeds, so this was very much a four-point affair for both sides.

Almost 60,000 fans flocked to Old Trafford for this contest. We were out for a double over Leeds; they were out to show that they could turn the tables and improve their own claims to the title prize. In the end, the game was almost an anti-climax, for we ran Leeds ragged. Three minutes, and we were ahead through Stewart Houston; 43 minutes, and Stuart Pearson scored our second; 63 minutes, and Gerry Daly put the issue beyond doubt. Leeds did manage two goals in a two-minute burst, right at the end of the game, but even they couldn't manage a third, in the one minute left.

On the day that we gave Leeds United the championship-style treatment, our title rivals were also doing their stuff. Goals by Stan Bowles and Mick Leach spurred Queen's Park Rangers to stay out in front at Goodison Park, although it was a game in which Everton played well enough to have deserved some reward for their efforts.

There was shock news from the Baseball Ground, where Derby County were taking on Norwich, conquerors of Liverpool at Anfield and Leeds at Elland-road . . . for the Canaries went into the lead for a spell. But Derby, stung by this reverse, made sure that Norwich would not be springing yet another away shock result, as they hammered three goals past the men from Carrow-road, to maintain their own challenge for the First Division championship.

Liverpool, the team who had got the job of playing away without conceding goals down to a fine art, also maintained their record, by pulling off a 1-0 victory against Birmingham at St. Andrew's, and so, despite the tremendous win we had achieved against Leeds – who had had an impressive record in previous appearances on our ground – the position remained pretty much as you were, at the top of the First Division table.

It was March 13 – unlucky for some, but not for the main title rivals – and this was how the table read, starting at the top: Queen's Park Rangers, Liverpool, Manchester United, Derby County and Leeds United. Rangers had played 35 matches, and collected 47 points; Liverpool were two points behind, but had a game in hand; Manchester United were also two points adrift . . . but we had two matches in hand on Rangers; and Derby, like ourselves and Liverpool, were on the 45-point mark, after having played 34 games. Leeds were trailing, with 40 points, but they had two games in hand on Rangers, so they weren't quite out of it yet.

How many points was it going to take to win the championship of the First Division? – People were beginning to say that the target must be at least 60 points. And some of the men involved in the title fight were doing quite a bit of talking about their own side's chances. Dave Mackay, who had added Leighton James to his talent-packed team, at a cost of £300,000, was making no secret of his belief that Derby could and would claim the title.

Rangers manager Dave Sexton, too, was quietly proclaiming his confidence in his team's ability to do the trick.

Liverpool boss Bob Paisley and United manager Tommy Docherty, on the other hand, were playing it cool – especially The Doc, who kept on saying that United had surprised him by their progress, and that he really didn't feel they were quite equipped to race into the lead and snatch the prize. I suppose that reflected the mood of most of us at Old Trafford, too, for while we knew the chance was there, we didn't bother our heads too much about the glittering prize itself.

We were happy enough to keep on going out and playing each game as it came along, maintaining our style and taking what came. If, at the end, we finished up with one of the honours, all well and good; but for the moment, sufficient unto the day, as they say. And that, without any question, is exactly the right attitude to take, when you have to slog through 42 matches in a season.

There was no denying that the situation was gripping the interest of every fan in the country, though, for not one of the teams could pull clear . . . yet not one of them was cracking, either, despite the pressure and the pace. The results one Saturday towards the end of March bore this out to the full. It was a day when Rangers, still the leaders, won with a David Webb goal at Stoke . . . and the rest of the challengers scored away wins, too.

Leeds kept alive their slender hopes by scoring a 3-1 victory over Everton at Goodison Park; Derby County went to Ayresome Park and chalked up a two-goal win over Middlesbrough; Liverpool, who had conceded only nine goals in 18 matches on opponents' grounds, went to Carrow-road and stole a 1-0 victory through David Fairclough, a precocious, red-headed teenager who had burst upon the scene as a marksman who almost never missed.

But Norwich manager John Bond had some hard words to say about Liverpool, after that victory. He made no bones about it – he didn't like their style, and he didn't feel it would be good for English football, if they eventually became League champions. John Bond preferred the sort of excitement generated by teams such as Queen's Park Rangers and Manchester United.

Well, we certainly generated excitement at St James's Park, that Saturday afternoon. While our rivals were all winning their away matches, we were in the thick of a seven-goal feast – and, finally, just coming out on top. Stuart Pearson struck for Manchester United after just 12 minutes; and Newcastle's John Bird put through his own goal, three minutes after that.

We were cock-a-hoop, of course, with the scent of victory in our nostrils. But Micky Burns scored for Newcastle after 17 minutes, Malcolm Macdonald levelled the score just inside the half-hour . . . and four minutes before half-time, Alan Gowling – who at one time played for Manchester United – sent the Magpies in with a 3-2 lead. No wonder the 41,000 spectators were buzzing with anticipation, as we resumed the battle, after our 10-minute break.

It was neck or nothing for us, as we started the second half, and we couldn't have had a greater morale-booster than the one Newcastle defender Pat Howard gave us, four minutes after the restart. For, like Bird in the first half, he put the ball through his own goal – and that was the moment we really became convinced there was no way we were going to lose this game. Just inside the hour, Stuart Pearson scored his second goal for us, and it turned out to be the clincher. Afterwards both sides had to admit that some bad goals had been conceded, but we went home happy enough with the knowledge that we had still finished up with just one more goal to show for our efforts than had our opponents.

We were one point behind Rangers, the leaders, and we had a match in hand. Liverpool were on 47 points, one behind us, and they had played 35 games, like ourselves. So had fourth-placed Derby, who trailed Liverpool only on goal average. And the following Saturday, all the title challengers were at home, so they were all expected to add two more points apiece to their tally. They did just that – Derby beat Birmingham, Liverpool beat Burnley, Rangers beat Manchester City, and United beat Middlesbrough, scoring three goals in a 10-minute spell to shatter the hopes of the men from Ayresome Park.

We had to wait an hour, before Gerry Daly planted home goal No.1 from the penalty spot; then David McCreery scored a second, and Gordon Hill hammered home our third. So we were all still going at it hammer and tongs . . . even Leeds, still hanging on grimly in fifth place, showed that they were not finished, by sticking three goals past Arsenal at Elland-road. It was Rangers 51 points, United and Derby County 50, Liverpool 49. United and Liverpool still had a game apiece in hand, as well.

The following week, Rangers and Liverpool each had three games to go; Derby and Leeds were four matches apiece off the finishing post; and Manchester United had five games still to play. But while Rangers were handing out a hiding to Middlesbrough, and Liverpool and Leeds were drawing their matches away from home, Derby County were losing a seven-goal thriller at Maine-road against Manchester City . . . and Manchester United, unable to do themselves a good turn, were taking a three-goal pasting from Ipswich at Portman-road.

Yet in spite of that disappointing defeat, we felt that we could still show at the end, for we clearly had a shout – five points behind Rangers, four behind Liverpool, and with two matches in hand on each of them. There was no doubt about it, though : the crunch was coming, and it was going to be fascinating for the onlookers, as they waited to see which, if any, of the championship challengers would finally crack.

The tension was terrific, and the moment you walked off the field after having completed your own game, you were anxiously inquiring what your rivals had done. And the answer, it seemed, was always the same . . . they had done as well as yourselves. Or, if you had dropped a point, so had they.

It was still virtually impossible to separate the main title rivals, and it was becoming clear that we were all going to have to consider what goal average could mean, in the final analysis. Points alone might not be sufficient to ensure that you carried off the prize.

On Saturday, April 14, Liverpool went to the top, with a 5-3 home win over Stoke at Anfield. Norwich, where we had drawn a few weeks earlier, put the skids under Queen's Park Rangers with a 3-2 win at Carrow-road. Derby could do no better than draw 2-2 at home against Leicester, and Manchester United scraped a somewhat fortunate 2-1 victory over Everton at Old Trafford. As Rangers manager Dave Sexton had recently observed, after his team had won at Everton, the top clubs were running out of matches, and the team which eventually claimed the title would just have to keep on winning every remaining game.

Now Leeds knew they would not finish as champions, because with two games left, they were five points adrift of Queen's Park Rangers. Derby, for whom nothing had gone right since their FA Cup semi-final defeat against us, could muster 57 points, if they won every one of their three matches – but Liverpool, already on 56 points, would have to lose their last two games, and as we all knew, they were highly unlikely to surrender the final four points, even though they had to visit Manchester City and the Wolves. At that stage, they were leading Rangers by a point. And now it looked a three-horse race, because Manchester United, with 52 points and four games left, could overhaul their rivals, if things went right for them.

Things didn't go right, however. The game that killed

our chances stone dead was played at Old Trafford in mid-week, and it was against a team which had caused us trouble on more than one occasion before. Stoke City. After a win against Burnley at Turf Moor, which took our tally to 54 points, we knew that victory over Stoke was vital. Liverpool had beaten Stoke on April 17, Rangers had beaten Arsenal on April 19, and that same day, Liverpool had gone to Maine-road and won.

Rangers had 57 points, and their final game of the season – at home, against Leeds – to play; Liverpool had postponed their last fixture, at Molineux, to May 4, and they were sweating it out on the 58-point mark. United's game against Stoke was on April 21, and we had matches left at Leicester and at home to Manchester City. If we beat Stoke and won at Leicester on April 24, it could all hinge on the night Liverpool met Wolves and United met Manchester City.

We started off brightly enough against Stoke, and threatened to over-run them in the early stages. Peter Shilton kept them in the game with a couple of good saves, yet it seemed that, eventually, a goal must come for United. But Stoke were nothing, if not stubborn, and when half-time came, with the score still 0-0, it left us with just 45 minutes to crack the opposition. Typically, we flung every-thing into attack, risking being caught on the break; and as the final few minutes loomed, we pushed everyone up into the assault.

That was when Stoke caught us out – and they scored the only goal of the game, with something like five minutes left. Alan Bloor, one of the City back-four men, got the goal, and if it wasn't the clearest-cut goal I have ever seen, it came at a time which could not have been worse for us. We sensed that our battle to finish as League champions had come to a full stop; and so it had. Ironically, that was our first defeat in the League at Old Trafford right through the season.

So the quest for the championship had been narrowed

down to two clubs, Liverpool and Queen's Park Rangers. We knew that we were destined to finish third, and after losing at Leicester and beating Manchester City – that was the night Liverpool made sure of the title – that was how things worked out. Those defeats by Stoke and Leicester left us with just one ambition – winning the FA Cup.

Suddenly, Manchester United could lose out on everything – and so could Lou Macari. Two little words could have great significance when I looked back over my short career in English football. I had said 'Yes' to Manchester United, and seen my dreams of winning a League-championship medal vanish; and now I knew that I could wind up as a loser a second time, in the final of the FA Cup. I had said 'No' to Liverpool . . . and there they were, one match away from the championship, and in the final of the UEFA Cup. Somehow, it all seemed to me to be ominous.

I had a few moments of wry reflection, but I knew it was no use feeling sorry for myself. I had made my decision on a January day three years previously, and there was no going back. Not that I really would have wanted to change things, because during my short spell at Old Trafford I had come to realise that Manchester United were, in every sense, a great club, and I felt that I had played my part in their emergence as a First Division force again. We were still in the final of the FA Cup, and we would qualify for the UEFA Cup, even if we failed at Wembley.

Away back in January, I hadn't really been dreaming about playing in the final of the FA Cup. We were going flat-out to win each game as it came along, and the excitement of being among the leaders of the First Division was enough, as it was. Our first engagement in the FA Cup didn't create tremendous excitement outside Manchester, either, because we were drawn at home against Oxford United, one of the strugglers in the Second Division. We might have played better, or maybe it was Oxford who raised their game for the occasion, in front of 41,000 people, and in the atmosphere of our famous ground; but at the end of 90 minutes, at least we had accomplished what we had set out to do: three goals had been scored, and we had notched two of them.

We didn't achieve that victory without a scare, though, because Derek Clarke, one of the footballing brothers, put Oxford ahead right on the half-time whistle, so it seemed a shock result might be on. But we returned the compliment as soon as we kicked off again, through our penalty king, Gerry Daly, and we added the interest seven minutes later, when we were awarded another spot-kick, because again Gerry made no mistake.

Everton, Burnley, Sheffield United – these three First Division clubs had made their exit; Middlesbrough, Queen's Park Rangers and Birmingham were shortly to go out of the competition in replays; and so were Aston Villa, who had held Southampton to a 1-1 draw at The Dell. Indeed, the Saints survived on their own ground only by courtesy of a last-minute equaliser from Hughie Fisher, so Wembley, at that time, must have seemed a mirage for them.

There had to be some more First Division casualties, when the fourth-round ties were played, because Liverpool were drawn at Derby (conquerors of Everton in round three), Newcastle (who had seen off Rangers in a replay) were at Coventry, and Ipswich were at home to Wolves. We were at home, too, against a side from a lower division for the second time in succession . . . Peterborough United, who were bidding boldly for a promotion place.

The Third Division club were managed by a former Manchester United player, Noel Cantwell, and he admitted he was thrilled to be bringing his team to the ground where he had taken part in so many big games. Noel was eager for his lads to go out and enjoy their football on what was, for them, a big occasion; and that echoed our own sentiments. We wanted the 'Posh' players to enjoy themselves, too – just so long as we enjoyed the proceedings even more, by recording a victory.

We took a bit of a gamble by playing Alex Stepney in goal, because he had ricked his back only the day before the tie, and he was having treatment to clear up the trouble until an hour or two before kick-off time. We didn't broadcast the news about the injury, but Tommy Docherty took the precaution of pulling Paddy Roche out of the reserves, and had him standing by . . . just in case. But when the time came for United's players to go on the field, Alex was in our line-up; Tommy Docherty had decided to take a chance on his getting through the game, and the gamble turned out to be justified.

It wasn't too stern a contest for us, as it happened, because Alex Forsyth gave us the lead after only eight minutes, and in another five minutes Sammy McIlroy had made it two for United. Our opponents pulled a goal back through John Cozens, with ten minutes to go to half-time, and Alex Stepney justified his inclusion when he prevented Cozens from snatching another goal, before we erased any lingering fears of a shock result by making it 3-1 shortly after play had been going for an hour. Not for the last time in our Cup campaign, as it turned out, Gordon Hill was our marksman.

So we went into round five . . . just like Southampton, who – having seen off Aston Villa in their replay – had despatched Blackpool with a 3-1 win at The Dell. Leicester were our next hurdle, and they were really rated as a Cup-fighting side; in addition, they had home advantage. But we went to Filbert-street with that positive outlook which had served us so well during the season. Now, we reasoned, was no time to change.

The goal I scored after only seven minutes' play gave me one of the greatest kicks I've had, since I moved into English football. The goal Gerry Daly tucked away after thirty-three minutes doubled my delight, and sparked off a brief thought about whom we might meet in the sixth round. And, of course, after that there were only ninety minutes to Wembley . . .

But nobody in the United side allowed himself to be sidetracked from the job in hand, which was making sure we didn't throw away our advantage, and while Bob Lee reduced the arrears, after an hour's play, United finished the game still leading 2-1, and good value for money in their moment of victory. The rest of the fifth-round ties had by no means been settled, for Sunderland and Stoke, Southampton and West Brom, and Newcastle and Bolton had to settle replays, while Norwich and Bradford City's fifth-round tie had been rearranged, for the following Wednesday.

But when all the matches had been played and replayed, the eight teams still left in the competition were Manchester United, Derby County, Southampton, Crystal Palace, Newcastle United, Wolves, Bradford City and Sunderland. And it was quite remarkable how many of those clubs were beginning to have 'double vision.'

United and Derby, as two of the top clubs in the First Division, had their sights on a championship-FA Cup double; Sunderland and Southampton had their sights on promotion to the First Division, as well as Wembley; Newcastle United had their ambitions, too – a return to Wembley for the second time during the season, to see if they could make up for the disappointment of having lost the League Cup against Manchester City. And Crystal Palace, going strongly in the Third Division, wanted a promotion place, as well as the FA Cup – which their manager, Malcolm Allison, claimed they were fated to win.

I don't think anyone wanted Manchester United and Derby County to be paired together, at that stage of the tournament – the right setting, people felt, would be Wembley itself . . . other teams permitting. When the draw was made, Bradford City, who had upset people's calculations with their victory at Norwich, were drawn at home against Southampton, Derby were set to tangle with Newcastle at the Baseball Ground, Sunderland were scheduled to meet Crystal Palace – who had knocked out Leeds and Chelsea – at Roker Park. And Manchester United had to take on Wolves at Old Trafford. So there was plenty to interest everybody, in that little lot . . . and quite a few ifs and buts, when it came to forecasting how things would go.

Bradford City fought valiantly enough against the Saints, but a goal from one of United's former players, Jim McCalliog, took Southampton through to the semi-finals. Derby, with two goals from Bruce Rioch, and a goal apiece from Henry Newton and Charlie George, saw off Newcastle, despite two goals in reply from Alan Gowling, another ex-Old Trafford player. Alan Whittle, who once starred for Everton, was the marksman who shattered the Sunderland dreams of a return to Wembley, where they had won the Cup against Leeds in 1973. And Manchester United? – We were the one side which failed to settle the issue at the first time of asking. Indeed, for a few minutes, it looked as if Wolves would spring the shock result of the round.

They were seeking an odd kind of double, for they were bang in trouble at the foot of the First Division. Only Sheffield United lay below them. So for Wolves, the double was one of securing First Division safety, as well as winning the FA Cup. And although they came to Old Trafford as under-dogs, they got in the first blow, when John Richards scored, after fifty-eight minutes.

With more than 59,000 people roaring us on, we were stung into throwing everything at the Wolves, and the impetus of our attacks forced them back on to the defensive. We had lost a goal against the run of play, but we made no mistake about redressing the balance, for it took us only nine minutes, after that Richards goal, to get on terms, and Gerry Daly, whose name has cropped up so often when I have mentioned goals, was the man on the mark.

But try as we might, after the encouragement of that equaliser, we couldn't polish off our opponents with another goal, and we had to settle for a final scoreline of 1-1, and a replay at Molineux the following Tuesday. The question some people were asking, of course, was: had Manchester United blown their chances? – That replay against the Wolves turned out to provide the perfect answer from our point of view, even though I didn't get through the ninety minutes of the game. I had started the match less than 100 per cent fit – as manager Tommy Docherty has said elsewhere, it was a gamble – and as time went on, it became clear that I was only aggravating the injury. So early in the second half, I pulled out.

But it was a match that had everything – thrills, goals, and an extra-time finale. The gate of close on 44,500 meant that the two matches between the sides had produced attendance figures topping 100,000 . . . and while the Wolves fans were in the majority at Molineux, there were plenty of supporters who had driven down the motorway from Manchester, so we knew we were not on our own.

The last time United had met Wolves in an FA Cup-tie at Molineux, it was Tommy Docherty's baptism of Cup football with the Manchester club, and Wolves had won that game by the only goal. Since then, we had scored two League victories over them. When Wolves went ahead in the replay, their fans were in full cry; when it was 2-0, the writing seemed on the wall for United.

But a turning point came when Stuart Pearson headed the ball into the Wolves net, and as we lined up for the restart, you could sense that our opponents were beginning to wonder if this was the beginning of a rescue operation for United. Yet I'll give credit to Wolves for the way they kept on trying to retain the mastery over us – and possibly they would have held on to win, if they had had that vital stroke of luck in the second half, when Steve Kindon hammered in a shot which looked a goal all the way. But the ball smashed against a post, and rebounded almost twenty yards. And after that let-off, we got a grip on things and Brian Greenhoff equalised.

The game still see-sawed back and forth, but there was no doubting what was going to happen, and the longer play went on, the more you could sense that Wolves realised there was going to be only one outcome: a United victory. We were simply not in the mood to return home defeated, and when Sammy McIlroy tucked the ball away for the winner, he raced away from the Wolves goal and turned a somersault in sheer delight, before being mobbed by his joyful team-mates.

The thrills, the quality of the football from both teams, the sheer excitement and drama of that game would not have disgraced a final at Wembley stadium, and as the United players walked off the park at the finish, you could only feel a sneaking sense of sympathy with the Wolves lads. They had made a game of it right to the end, and they were sporting enough to accept their defeat with smiles, as if to acknowledge that they had had their chances, and failed to profit by them. Which was true enough.

But deep down, they must have felt sickened; I know I would have done, had my team gone two goals up in a replay at home, after having done the hard bit away, and still finished on the losing end. But there was no dispute about it – Manchester United had earned their semi-final place.

Even when I was playing in Scottish football with Celtic, I had learned enough about Manchester United to know that they had acquired a tremendous reputation in the FA Cup competition, although their last success at Wembley had been in season 1962-63, when they defeated Leicester City 3-1. In those days, the heroes of the United supporters were Denis Law, David Herd – who scored two goals against Leicester – and Bobby Charlton.

Now United were almost through to Wembley once again – and the new-look side was taking the Old Trafford club into its 11th semi-final since the war. The last semi-final occasion had begun at Hillsborough, when Manchester's United met the United from Leeds. Then, six years earlier, the game had ended in a scoreless draw, and the two teams contested the affair again, this time at Villa Park. Even though that match went to extra time, not a goal had been scored after a total of 210 minutes' play, and it took a third meeting, at Burnden Park, to settle the issue. A goal from Billy Bremner knocked Manchester United off the trail, just as they could almost see the twin towers of Wembley.

United's post-war semi-final appearances had been against Leeds (1970), Everton (1966), Leeds (1965), West Ham (1964), Southampton (1963), Tottenham (1962), Fulham (1958), Birmingham (1957), Wolves (1949) and Derby County (1948). Now here we were, having just beaten Wolves, who had contested a semi-final twenty-seven years previously, and looking forward to meeting Derby County, whom United had last met in a semi-final twenty-eight years ago. We hoped that it was a lucky omen, too, for on March 13, 1948, the United team of those days had scored a 3-1 victory over Derby . . . and at Hillsborough, too. What was more, a forward called Pearson – Stan Pearson – had scored a hat-trick for United.

So it was Southampton v Crystal Palace, and Manchester United v Derby County, for the right to appear at Wembley on May 1. And if everyone was expressing some regret about United and Derby having to clash before the final itself, at least people all round the country were able to anticipate a showgame at Hillsborough. April 3 was quite an occasion, too; for in the morning, at Anfield, championship challengers Liverpool met and defeated their great derby-game rivals, Everton; and in the afternoon the Grand National was being run at Aintree. We should have been meeting Manchester City in a League match at Old Trafford, but our semi-final date meant that was a pleasure which had to be deferred.

There was just one snag, so far as I was concerned – I wasn't able to play against Derby. I had limped out of the replay at Molineux, and I spent the weeks before the semi-final striving to regain full fitness. As the days went by, I began to realise that I was fighting a losing battle, and even though manager Tommy Docherty said he was willing to wait until the last minute for a fitness decision on me, I knew that I wasn't going to make it.

It was a terrible disappointment to me, and some people felt that Derby's all-round experience might prove too much for a United side which needed the know-how of Lou Macari. But, like the manager and the rest of my team-mates, I knew that young David McCreery, who had stepped into my place, would give a good account of himself. And he did.

If United had spent a great deal of money on players such as myself, Stuart Pearson, Alex Forsyth and Martin Buchan, Derby had plunged even more heavily. The four of us cost a total of around £600,000; Dave Mackay had splashed half that sum on one man, Welsh international winger Leighton James, signed from Burnley. Add players like Rod Thomas, Bruce Rioch, Francis Lee, Colin Todd, David Nish, Archie Gemmill, Charlie George and Henry Newton, and you had a million-pound line-up.

To be fair about it, Derby County had a key man missing, too, when they walked out on the park for the semi-final at Hillsborough. Charlie George, who had scored some vital goals for them right through the season, and who had blossomed as a player in top form since he joined Derby, was a casualty. And there can be no doubt that, on the day, they missed him. More, maybe, than Manchester United missed me. But, having made allowance for Charlie's absence, it has to be said – and manager Dave Mackay later admitted it himself – that Derby never really raised their game to suit the occasion.

With all the wealth of talent in their side, and the players with such vast experience at international level, as well as at club level, Derby should have been the team best-equipped to cope, to banish nerves and show exactly why they were one of the outstanding sides in the country. But frankly, they didn't even begin to put their game together; it seemed as if they had to spend most of their time trying to chase the Red shadows from Old Trafford.

And for Manchester United, two of the star performers were players who had cost comparatively modest sums – little more than £100,000 between them – and were still learning what life at the top was all about. Wingers Steve Coppell and Gordon Hill. Indeed, every member of the United side played his part, but Gordon Hill's was the name on the tongues of most people, by the time the game had ended. He was almost impudent, at times, as he took men on and beat them – and when it came to displaying how to take scoring chances, he demonstrated that he packs a wallop. His were the goals that sank Derby County without trace, and left them thoroughly demoralised.

And from the moment they walked off the field defeated at Hillsborough, it seemed, Derby could do little else right, as the season reached its climax. Their hopes of a League title-FA Cup double had vanished, and soon they had to admit that the championship, too, was beyond their grasp. I don't want to rub salt into an old wound, but I have to say that Leighton James, the £300,000 winger whom many people expected to be a match-winner, rarely showed that afternoon; and Dave Mackay's claim that he had the most talented team in the country could surely be questioned, after the way they were destroyed – and failed to destroy – opposition which, basically, was still learning a lot about life at the top.

Derby had given a hiding to Real Madrid, in the European

Cup-tie at the Baseball Ground – and been punished in return, when they played the second leg in Spain. They had
players who had already tasted the joy of a League-
championship success, players who had acquired a wealth
of international experience. But on the day when it mattered
most, Derby failed to live up to their own high expectations.
And Manchester United went on to meet Southampton in
the FA Cup final at Wembley.

Having said my piece about Derby's failure at Hillsborough, you might wonder what excuses I'm going to put
forward for Manchester United's defeat against Southampton at Wembley. I'm not – I'm just going to admit that,
again on the day, we didn't do ourselves justice, either.
Frankly, I would much rather United had been meeting
Derby at Wembley, instead of the Saints, because I felt that
in almost every way, we were on a hiding to nothing. We
were made the red-hot favourites to win the final; and Southampton didn't do anything to destroy the illusion that they
were indeed the under-dogs. In fact, as I said before the final,
I feel that Southampton made the most of a confidence trick.

I'm not crying, now that it's too late; and I'm not blaming
the Saints for the way they prepared for the occasion. They
did what was right for them. Southampton simply thrived
on being called the under-dogs . . . they accepted, or appeared to accept, what people said about Manchester United
being the favourites, and they knew that if anyone was
going to be under pressure because of this favourites' tag,
it would be us. Had we been in their situation, I would
have wanted to play it exactly the same way.

I felt that Manchester United had to achieve the impossible – win by something like four clear goals and turn
on a display of footballing magic for the whole ninety
minutes. Only that would be sufficient; anything less, and
we would stand to be criticised. The spotlight was so firmly
on Manchester United that Southampton could afford to
relax. If they played and lost, then that was only what

F

people had expected; if they did better than people expected, and took us to extra time, or even won, then they would get more than their share of praise . . . and, equally, United would get more than their share of condemnation. The Saints knew most people rated United certain winners, before the ball had been kicked; any other result, and it would be classed as a sensation.

As I battled to get fully fit for the final, I mulled over the publicity and the attitude of the critics. And the more I thought about it, the less I liked the build-up. Haunting me, too, was the memory of that 1971 League Cup final, when Glasgow Celtic crashed 4-1 to Partick Thistle at Hampden Park. Celts then couldn't be beaten; they had only to turn up to collect the League Cup. And I felt that Manchester United were in a similar sort of situation. Sadly, my fears were to prove only too well founded.

Looking back, and trying to be objective, I think it's a fair comment to say that Manchester United didn't go blowing their own trumpet, and claiming that they were sure-fire winners. Chairman Louis Edwards appealed to all our supporters to be on their best behaviour at Wembley – and he acknowledged, as he made his appeal, that it was a final Manchester United could lose. Manager Tommy Docherty also played it in a low key, saying merely that he hoped we would play as well as we had done against such sides as Derby County, and that this would be good enough to win the game for us.

We weren't strung up by nerves, although we had our share of butterflies. We were only too well aware that there is many a slip . . . and, unfortunately, if we were the ones who did slip up, we would be vulnerable to fierce criticism. The fact that we had forfeited our chance of winning the League title, with our pre-final defeats against Stoke and Leicester, had not been lost upon people, and in the last few hours before Wembley day dawned, the doubts began to be expressed about United. It was a strangely unreal sort of situation, and I know that several of our players wanted to get all the pre-match ballyhoo behind them and get on with the game.

When it did get under way, we started to push the ball around, and for the first ten minutes or so, I really began to revive my hopes that it was going to be our day, after all. We almost scored two goals, in that opening flourish, and there seemed to be more than a touch of desperation about Southampton's play. There was, perhaps, also a hint of fear. But as the game wore on, and we had still failed to breach their defence, I began to sense that it was going to be the Stoke match all over again. The same sort of pattern was beginning to emerge.

Experienced men like Peter Osgood, Mike Channon and Jim McCalliog finally started to make things tick for the Saints, and I have to admit that right through the game, Southampton had big men at the back in every way, in Peter Rodrigues, David Peach, Jim Steele and Mel Blyth. There was vast experience and know-how running right through the Saints side, as anyone with intelligence knew before the final, and when Southampton began visibly to muster increasing confidence, the signs were there that they could snatch victory.

If a goal is awarded by the referee, it stands, whether you think it's offside or not. And I'm not going to start any arguments now about the one which Bobby Stokes tucked away for the Saints. I shall simply say that it came late in the game, just as I had feared – too late for our players to make an effective reply. We had run around until we were leg-weary, and when you see your best efforts hitting the bar, or going narrowly past the post, when you see the opposing goalkeeper having ninety minutes' worth of luck in the opening minutes, then making his own luck at different stages of the game, there comes a point where you start to believe that no matter what, it's not going to be your day.

I sensed this, quite a while before the Saints got the goal that won the Cup. United never ceased trying to claw their way back into the game, but time was running out. Had we scored even once in that opening flourish, when we had Southampton rocking a bit, I am convinced we would have justified that tag as favourites. But as the game wore on, something told me, deep down, that Southampton had weathered the storm, and they could snatch victory in the end.

They caught us out as we were still striving to get that elusive goal which could have opened the floodgates for us. And once they had gone ahead, at such a late stage, they were not going to be denied. Players such as Osgood, McCalliog, Channon, Rodrigues, Steele and company would see to that – they knew exactly what to do to retain what they had wrung from us. And I would not want anyone to think that I am giving Southampton little credit for their performance.

They did the job in the best way they possibly could, and they did it effectively. I would be the last to deny them the glory of their victory, and they were certainly right to savour it to the full. For they had proved so many people wrong. Our sorrow was demonstrated without the need for words, in the picture of Brian Greenhoff, who had given everything, like his team-mates, kneeling and shedding tears when the final whistle blew.

One thing on which everyone was agreed afterwards: Manchester United may have been the beaten favourites, but they lost with tremendous dignity. The players and the manager took defeat on the chin – and stayed on their feet to go forward and congratulate the winners. Tommy Docherty, I know, was choking back his utter disappointment as he spoke about the game, and saluted his opposite number, Lawrie McMenemy, and the Saints players.

And if there was another consolation for us, it was in the reception we received when we returned to Manchester.

Our supporters remained loyal, and made us feel that we
had not let them down. One more thing: Manchester United
are young enough and good enough to get to Wembley again
– and to win the FA Cup. When they do, I fervently hope
that I shall be a member of that side. One loser's medal is
enough for me.

13 Confounding The Critics

Criticism from outside – and self-criticism too, for that
matter – can be a healthy influence, sometimes. On other
occasions, it can be difficult to distinguish if the criticism is
made with the best of motives, or if it is tinged with a shade
of jealousy. When a player, a manager or a club achieves the
pinnacle of success in Soccer, there is always someone ready
to criticise, and when a football club achieves the stature of
genuine greatness, then it becomes a sitting target, should
the standards it has set begin to slip even slightly.

Through the years, Manchester United have overcome
many difficulties. They were not always a wealthy club –
in the dim and distant past, there was the threat of extinc-
tion, because of financial problems, for instance. There was
the Munich air disaster, which virtually obliterated a team.
And there was the descent into the Second Division, in the
early 1970's. Perhaps Manchester United were fortunate
in one respect: when they appointed Tommy Docherty as
their manager, they chose a man who had known the highlights and the low points of Soccer . . . a man who could
give as good as he got.

I have referred elsewhere to the transition which took
place after Tommy Docherty had arrived at Old Trafford.
On the surface – and in retrospect – it seems that the transition was effected smoothly, and without any great fuss,
even though The Doc had always been noted for his
incisive style. Yet even he, I am sure, must have wrestled
for some long and maybe lonely hours, as he weighed up
what he felt needed to be done at Old Trafford. It's one

thing to go out and buy new players; it's another to undertake a pruning operation at the same time.

A few months before my arrival at Old Trafford, Glasgow Celtic had played there in Bobby Charlton's testimonial match, and it was becoming clear that Bobby's magnificent career was coming to a close at United. He had been one of the stars during the club's glory years, and the mere mention of his name also produced thoughts of others who had been idols at Old Trafford. Think of Charlton, and you immediately thought of Denis Law and George Best.

Tommy Docherty had shown throughout his managerial career that he was prepared to give youth its fling, and while it might not always have brought quite as much success as he had hoped, he has never been a man for looking backwards. When he arrived at Old Trafford, the era of the great players of the 1960s was clearly coming to an end, and the big question in many people's minds was how The Doc would make the decisions, when the time came.

There were shock waves when it was announced that Denis Law had been given a free transfer, and when he joined Manchester City, it was natural that people should speculate on whether United had done the right thing, after all. When Denis began scoring goals for City, some people seemed to think that this was an embarrassment to Manchester United.

Tommy Docherty faced the critics, and gave his considered opinion. 'I am delighted that Denis is doing well for Manchester City . . . I hope he continues to play an important part for them.' Manchester United's manager didn't dodge the fact that the decision to free Denis had been a difficult one; but, he countered, it was one which had had to be made for Manchester United. 'We are at a stage in our development for rebuilding, and Denis is thirty-three,' he summed up.

Giving the man who had been 'king' at Old Trafford a free

transfer did not mean to say that Manchester United had thought Denis Law was finished. As The Doc reminded people: 'I was the man who brought him back into the Scotland team, only a short while before.' In Tommy Docherty's view, a free transfer did not mean that Denis Law was being snubbed by the club which had had such fine service from him; it was a gesture to help Denis find a new club 'on as generous terms as possible, because no fee is involved.'

Denis and another United stalwart, Tony Dunne, both benefited from the actions of Manchester United, because they were able to move on to other clubs without the worry as to whether or not transfer fees would prove a stumbling block to the continuance of their first-team careers. And with their departure, the way was paved for younger players to get their chance.

So Tommy Docherty began to mould the new-look Manchester United, but there were many other changes made, as the months went by under his managership. And while, as I said earlier, it may all have seemed to have gone smoothly, in the end, there were plenty of headaches along the way – and plenty of people who were ready to snipe at Manchester United.

The early months of 1974, as we battled for the second season in succession against relegation, were not happy ones for anyone at the club, especially after we suffered a fourth-round FA Cup knock-out on our own ground at the hands of Ipswich. In the third round, I scored the goal which disposed of Third Division Plymouth, but we gained little credit for that performance, and shortly after we had lost in the next round against Ipswich, United's manager was admitting that it was proving 'a worrying and disappointing season' for United.

By the time we played Leeds United at Old Trafford, we were at the foot of the First Division table, and The Doc was answering criticisms which had been made of our display earlier in the season at Elland-road. We had been taken to task for so-called spoiling tactics and rough play, and this sort of accusation, as our manager said, had been trotted out more than once when we had been involved in a match which had proved to be especially tight.

Tommy Docherty, like the players, resented such criticism, and he made no bones about his feelings. Criticism so far as our League position was concerned was justified; but The Doc felt that we were in danger of becoming the victims of what he called 'a witch-hunt', because, as he put it, 'a once-great team is not doing so well now.' He reckoned that people were over-eager to have a go at Manchester United purely because 'we are not what we were, our football is not so polished, and the results are not so good.' But if we had our critics, we also had our champions, and one of them was Plymouth manager Tony Waiters, who said that before the Cup-tie against us, he had been asked leading questions by people who wanted him to 'have a go' at United and to mock our lowly position in the First Division.

As Tommy Docherty said, the Plymouth boss was answering on our behalf from the other side of the fence. 'I wish a few more managers would wake up to what is happening,' said The Doc. 'Too many players are blackening our name unfairly. They make remarks about the way we play, and infer that we are a dirty team . . . and their quotes are printed.'

As United's manager reminded people, we were having to fight hard for our results; but most certainly we were NOT a dirty side. 'I am delighted to find that the Plymouth manager, at least, was alive to a problem with which I am only too familiar. I wish it wasn't so.'

From his early days at Old Trafford, too, Tommy Docherty was alive to the problems of crowd behaviour, and he didn't duck the issue when he admitted that Manchester United had had what he called 'some embarrassing moments' from some of the chanting at the Stretford End. But he also spoke up in the Stretford Enders' favour when he said that no one should question either the patience or the faith of the United followers. And patience and faith were qualities which both club and supporters needed, in the dark days immediately preceding relegation.

I remember the words of another First Division player, when his side was going through a bit of a rough spell. He said winning 'tended to be a bit of a habit . . . now losing has become a bit of a habit, and you find you just don't come back, if you go a goal or two behind.' He could easily have been talking about Manchester United, instead of his own club, for those words certainly applied to us, as we grappled with the task of steering clear of the Second Division. We didn't survive in the First Division, in the end, and that was good news to some people, as I am well aware.

For more years than many folk cared to remember, Manchester United had been in the habit of winning; so much so that people began to take it for granted – and not all of them felt kindly disposed towards the Old Trafford club. When United got into the habit of not winning, during their relegation season, it was a habit they found difficult to break. But break it we did, in the end, as we stormed through the Second Division campaign to claim promotion, and our return to the top flight, of course, posed more question marks – and provided more ammunition for some of the club's critics, as I mentioned earlier in this book.

However, I don't believe that anyone would dispute it – we confounded all our critics, when we went so close to winning the League championship and the FA Cup, during our first season back in Division One. And as that season wore on, the doubters clearly began to revise their opinions about the ability of Manchester United to make a stirring comeback. Tommy Docherty, who had shown many times during his career that he was prepared to take a gamble, found that his gambles had turned up trumps for Manchester United, by and large. And he has no need now to worry about the critics. Knowing him, though, I shouldn't imagine that he has ever lost a moment's sleep, in any event, about what other people have been thinking; perhaps his one nightmare was when we did fail to avoid relegation – and he soon put that behind him.

Still, it's always a pleasure to be proved right – especially when you can be big enough, as The Doc has been, to admit that on occasion you have also been wrong. And a lot of people who, at the start of our return to the First Division, had been expressing their reservations about our ability to cope, were saying so many nice things about Manchester United long before the end of that term.

One former Manchester United player who held up his hand was Don Givens, of Queen's Park Rangers. He admitted that before Rangers and United met in First Division combat, he had been a bit dubious about our record, and about the rave notices we had been receiving. He was honest enough to say he had thought United carried too many youngsters in their side, and that we were not as good as people were making out. We played and lost at Loftus-road, but after that match, Don had revised his opinions. He said he had been impressed by United generally, and especially by the way we kept trying to play football, right through the ninety minutes. By the end of that season, a lot of other people had commented favourably upon the fact that we concentrated on football, not feuding, and that we tried to attack and entertain wherever we were in action.

Don Givens did have one reservation – he doubted that we had the ability to carry off the First Division championship, largely because he felt we still lacked the necessary experience; but he believed we would finish in the top half-dozen . . . and it was a pleasure to prove him right. Don said what a lot of others had to admit in the end: that our brand of football was a credit to the First Division; by the time he had come up against us at close quarters, he was conceding that Manchester United didn't keep going merely on enthusiasm – we not only had the will to work for each other, but we had a team of genuine skill.

We got credit from the Leeds players, too, after our victory over them at Old Trafford; and our arch-rivals from across the way, Manchester City, were big enough to sing our praises. Their skipper, Mike Doyle, who had not exactly been noted for his pro-Manchester United views in the past, paid us compliments in a generous manner – and we knew he meant what he said.

Another of the Manchester City stars, winger Dennis Tueart, made the point that successful sides are often copied by others – and the more teams which try to copy the style of Manchester United, the better we shall like it, because don't forget that it always takes two teams to make a game. Furthermore, you know what they say about imitation being the most sincere form of flattery!

I think it was significant that so many players from other clubs expressed their admiration for Manchester United's style, too. Arsenal's Alan Ball said we had 'taken the First Division by the scruff of its neck'; Ian Ross, of Aston Villa, talked about our 'sheer enthusiasm, and the enjoyment United have given so many spectators'; and John Craven, of Coventry, said we had 'played it straight and simple, while the rest of us have tended to be carried away with tactics.'

From Derby and England centre-half Roy McFarland came this tribute: 'United have brought back so much good into the game, and given the public a taste for football once more.' Everton's Martin Dobson said we had been 'a credit to the game, wonderful to watch.' Billy Bremner, of Leeds, admitted we had been 'a revelation with our running capacity and skill. They have all-round teamwork, plus one of the best target men in the business, Stuart Pearson.'

Liverpool skipper Emlyn Hughes thought United had been 'fantastic, in the way they have come back into the First Division and played such good football', and Duncan Forbes, of Norwich, remarked that 'United have brought back the two-winger system, which is great for football.' Don Given's club-mate, Gerry Francis (who also is England's skipper) said: 'We thought we could play them (United) off the park. But they proved me wrong, with their unique brand of attacking football.'

One of the best midfield players in the country is Tony Currie. Leeds showed what they thought of him, when they paid Sheffield United something like £275,000 for the England international. And he showed what he thought about the other United from Manchester, when he said: 'They have given football a new lease of life, and other teams have followed them.'

Brian Greenhoff's 'big brother', Jimmy, who has done so much since he joined Stoke, was trying his hardest to put one across us when City played – and won – at Old Trafford, to dash our hopes of the First Division championship. But that didn't stop him singing our praises. 'Manchester United have swept teams aside by sheer energy; but their pace also tends to overshadow the tremendous skill in the side.'

No one would dispute that West Ham are one of the First Division's most attractive sides, and that Billy Bonds is one of the top players in our game. What did he have to say about Manchester United? – 'The most exciting team I've seen this season . . . their style is refreshing, and good for football.' And from a player who has long commanded admiration for his own, never-say-die style of football: 'United have brought a breath of fresh air to the game.' Yes, that was Mike Bailey, who tried so hard to help Wolves avoid the relegation fate which overtook us a few seasons ago.

So Manchester United have won applause not merely from the spectators, but from the professionals in the game

– in fact, from all sides, because the critics, too, joined in
the general admiration for what Manchester United had
tried to achieve with their brand of attacking, open football. As a professional myself, I appreciate a compliment
from a fellow-player – even if I have regrets about missing
out on the medals.

Of course, if Manchester United should slip from the
high standard they have set, we shall be open to criticism
once again. But there can be no question about one thing:
Tommy Docherty's team brought back the sort of football
which had graced the Old Trafford scene during the days of
the club's former greatness. And if we have won applause
from all sides, we have also won the unswerving support
of our own fans. It is true that the club has been worried
by a minority which has caused trouble, at times, but it
would be grossly unfair for anyone to castigate Manchester
United's supporters generally as hooligans.

When you can command crowds of 50,000 and more for
virtually every match you play on your own ground, and
double the gates of the clubs you are visiting, then I feel
that in this day and age, you are bound to find a few people
who go looking for trouble. I recall someone telling me
about a pre-season friendly between Huddersfield and
Barnsley at Oakwell a few seasons ago . . . the ground was
far from full, yet there were some so-called fans who were
more interested in punch-ups than in football. So trouble
doesn't erupt just when Manchester United and their fans
are in town. And I maintain that the solid core – by which
I mean up to 50,000 – of United's fans are people of whom
we, the players, can be proud. They all go to watch us win;
and the vast majority of them behave properly, whether
we win or lose.

And while I'm in full flow about the tremendous support
we do receive, home and away, I wonder how many other
First Division clubs could boast a following of no fewer
than 5,000 fans, when they travelled 200 miles or more for

a mid-week night match? – That happened, when we played at Norwich, during our first season back in the top flight.

And what happened, when we went to play at White Hart-lane against the Spurs? – Tottenham reserved their entire South End stand for the supporters of Manchester United. Our club received an allocation of 4,000 tickets for the terraces, and 2,600 tickets for seated accommodation. How many other clubs could command such support, when they are playing 200 miles away from their own ground?

It's no surprise when Manchester United announce that games at Old Trafford against the top teams such as Liverpool, Manchester City, Leeds United, Queen's Park Rangers and Derby County are all-ticket affairs; but possibly only Liverpool could claim to come close to us both in the number of fans and the amount of vocal support, when they are playing away from their own ground. I can assure you that when United are playing away, on grounds all round the country, the support we receive is so great that as we run out on the park and hear the cheers from our fans, we could be forgiven for thinking that we were playing a home match.

We have fans who travel to Old Trafford from every corner of Britain, too – they come from London, Scotland, Wales and from across the Irish Sea. We have supporters' branches all round the world, as well – and some of the fans from abroad make Old Trafford their first place of call, when they come to England on holiday. They sometimes save up especially to make the trip, just so that they can see Manchester United playing in a 'live' game.

There is a postman whose home city is Vienna – and yet he considers Manchester United to be 'his' club; he has appeared at Old Trafford for matches on several occasions, to my knowledge. Another Manchester United fan hails from Athens, and he had seen the team playing via television. When he came to England to study, he chose

Manchester as a base from which he could watch United in live action.

We have supporters – plenty of them – in the George Cross island of Malta. They enjoy seeing United in action, when our games are screened on Sunday-afternoon television, and I am told that while other English clubs are also popular in Malta, there is no question as to which club tops the lot – it's Manchester United. When Tommy Docherty went to Malta as a guest of the local United supporters' branch, he received an enthusiastic welcome, and I know he was tremendously impressed by the fervour of our fans who live on the sunny Mediterranean island.

So the magic of Manchester United is there for all to see, and we have every reason to be grateful to – and confident we can keep – our supporters, who have such a deep affection for the club. They kept faith with United, even during the season when we were relegated – the average home gate then was close on 43,000. That figure rose to more than 48,000 during our promotion season, and on our return to Division 1, we were playing almost every home game in front of 50,000-plus crowds . . . not to mention average gates of more than 35,000, when we were away from home.

By the time we had played Everton in mid-April, our home League gates during season 1975-76 had topped the million mark, and our three FA Cup-ties at Old Trafford had pulled in more than 156,000 fans – even though, of the opposition, only Wolves were a First Division club. It was little wonder that when we went to Wembley, our chairman, Mr Louis Edwards, and our manager spelled out the danger of fans travelling to London without having got tickets for the final.

When you consider that each of the clubs in the final gets an allocation of only 25,000 tickets, it can easily be seen that Manchester United could supply only half their regular customers with those precious slips of paper, for our average home attendance topped 54,000. United, and their supporters, thus found themselves in an impossible situation.

I can appreciate all the problems of allocating tickets for a game which would attract double the number of people the ground can hold. Let's face it, the FA Cup final presents the same poser year by year –twice as many fans would be flocking down Wembley Way, if the stadium could accommodate 200,000 people, instead of 100,000.

But I have to agree with manager Tommy Docherty: when a club consistently attracts crowds of more than 50,000 for its home games, an allocation of only 25,000 tickets for the Cup final seems laughable. Still, that's how the system works, and until a new and bigger stadium is built, or clubs receive an allocation based on their average support, there is nothing to be done about it.

Incidentally, I think there is a strong case to be made out for all-ticket games, when Manchester United are the visitors even for ordinary League matches. I'm thinking of the crowd problems which arose when we played West Ham at Upton Park – the game was held up for close on 20 minutes in the second half. On that occasion, it seems the West Ham supporters, in the main, were the ones responsible for the trouble, for the majority of the people arrested or ejected from the ground were fans of the Hammers.

But the point I'm making is that West Ham didn't declare this an all-ticket game; and experience has proved that when the fans have to get tickets, it's easier to ensure that the rival supporters are kept apart. I remember that when we played at Norwich, the police kept a close eye on things, and the United fans were the first to leave the ground, so as to lessen the risk of incidents. It's a great pity, of course, that clubs have to endure such problems, but we have to live in the world as it is, and not as we would like it to be.

I know United are as concerned as anyone that their supporters should not cause trouble, and in my view, making a game all-ticket is a sensible precaution, when you know you can expect an influx of visiting fans. Segregating the rival supporters becomes a far easier proposition. United have been very conscious of that minority of trouble-makers whom the club refuses to call fans: at one stage, the players themselves volunteered to meet supporters and try to get the 'good behaviour' message across. Tommy Docherty has often praised the genuine supporters, but he has also been at pains to remind people that United are jealous of their high reputation, and that it is important the fans take the same line. And our chairman sent a special FA Cup-final message to everyone about the need for good behaviour at Wembley.

The United chairman admitted: 'It is sad that we should have to worry about this, but some of those who follow the club have let us down so often in the past that it is something which cannot be ignored. All we can do is hope everyone attending the game will go in a spirit of good sportsmanship, ready to cheer our team to victory . . . and if the day goes against us, then to give due credit to our opponents.' Well, it turned out to be a disappointing end for Manchester United, but the reputation of the club remained intact, as players and officials behaved impeccably . . . and I would like to give credit where it is due in another direction, too, because our supporters heeded the chairman's appeal. They did nothing to wreck the proceedings at Wembley, and they gave us all good cause to be proud of the way they rallied round.

14 A Winner's Medal Is The Answer

Football is a game where you can be up one day, and down the next; and opinions can change as swiftly as the wind blows. England, for example, finished the 1976 home-international tournament by losing to Scotland at Hampden Park, and they were given a bit of a slating for their performance. Yet one week later, although they had lost to Brazil in the United States, England were being applauded for their display; and after they had come back to defeat Italy — one of their direct opponents later in the year, when the qualifying rounds of the World Cup came along — England were being hailed as a team which could make a bold showing in the 1976 tournament in Argentina.

Everyone was agreed that England set problems for Brazil in their game in the US, and Don Revie's team could feel heartened by the tributes which were paid to them. Yet the players knew without needing to be told that they had still lost that game, in the dying minutes . . . and for them, the result must have stuck in their throats. For basically football is all about winning. And that's a theme which has run through the pages of this book, as you will be well aware by now.

I want to win medals with my club, and I want to be a member of a Scotland team which is successful. So perhaps you would like to know what I think about England, Scotland, and the international scene generally. For more years than we would care to admit, we — and by we, I mean the Scots — had a somewhat insular attitude towards Soccer. Maybe in the first place it was because we felt, deep down, that we could play the game better than anyone else, but one of the problems was that Scottish football was for ever losing its best players to clubs south of the Border. Every time a player began to make a name for himself, he would become the target for an English club, and over the years dozens of Scots have made the trek south.

Maybe we were a little resentful about the way our footballing talent was creamed off, but there was nothing the Scottish clubs could do about it, because finance was a vital consideration, and big transfer fees helped to keep many a Scottish club solvent. However, when it came to building a winning international side, the drain of players to England meant that there wasn't as much home-based talent – certainly not sufficient to enable Scotland to do themselves justice in the international arena.

Attempts were made to field an all-Scottish side, and many people north of the Border argued that players from clubs in England should not be chosen. Thankfully, as time went by, we came to realise, and more important still to accept, that just because a player had left Scotland to better himself with a crack English club, it didn't mean to say that he had deserted his country. So gradually the arguments against Scotland picking 'Anglos' petered out, and the name of the game became international football once more, with the objective victory.

In my time as a Scotland international, many players from English clubs have worn the blue jersey with distinction, and some of those players don't even speak with a truly Scottish accent. They qualified for international selection by virtue of being able to claim Scottish nationality – but once they donned the jersey, they were as eager to do well for Scotland as anyone who had been born and bred north of the Border.

Frankly, it would be ridiculous for Scotland to ignore the wealth of talent at her disposal, just because players had moved into English club football. You have only to think of the Scottish players at Old Trafford – men like Martin Buchan, Alex Forsyth, Jim Holton and myself – to recognise that the case for picking 'Anglos' is overwhelmingly strong. So we have got our priorities right, when we go for the best players available to represent Scotland.

Whether we have got our priorities right in another respect, though, I am not so sure. After Scotland's opening victories in the home internationals against Wales and Northern Ireland, the cry was 'Bring on the English!' And that battlecry was roared, full-throated, as the Scots met and mastered their old adversaries at Hampden Park. For the fans, it was a great occasion; for the Scotland players too, for that matter. But beating England is not the be-all and end-all of international football, and sometimes I am not so sure that we appreciate this.

There have been times when I have felt that England's footballers are motivated to succeed for their country, no matter what the opposition, while Scotland have regarded the annual match against England as THE game in which we must succeed. I think that perhaps our supporters heighten this impression, or even create it in the first place; yet I have no doubts that they get behind their team more than the England fans get behind theirs.

Scotland is a country with its own identity, yet Scotland is also like a village, where it seems everyone knows everyone else, and when it comes to giving the international football team backing the Scottish fans are more fervent than their English counterparts, and as loyal as any supporters in the world. More than once, England team-manager Don Revie has called for the vocal support of the fans . . . and, to be fair, their cheers and rallying calls have been heard clearly enough. But when Scotland go out to play in front of their supporters, team-manager Willie Ormond doesn't need to ask the fans to rally round – our supporters are in full cry from the start.

Scotland put up a fine performance in the finals of the

1974 World Cup; not many teams can claim that they were knocked out of a tournament without having lost a game. Between 1974 and 1976, there were problems for Scotland at international level, but by the time we had met and beaten England at Hampden Park in the 1976 international, you got the feeling that we were really on the right lines, so far as competing successfully against the world, and not just England, was concerned.

Not only did we have eleven players who were knitting together as a team unit; we had men in reserve who could come into the side and maintain the rhythm and effectiveness, and as of now I feel for the first time that Scotland have moulded a player-squad which could do better than England in World Cup competition.

Something tells me that the impact made by Tommy Docherty, when he took over as Scotland's team manager, put us on the road to international success and gave us the initial impetus; and Willie Ormond, who has had more than his fair share of worries, now seems to have built on a solid foundation and assembled a squad of players who can do themselves and Scotland justice against the rest of the world.

Competition against the best is essential, at international and club level, and there is always something to be learned from top-class opposition in every game. At club level, I believe that Manchester United's entry in the UEFA Cup competition provided a new and different experience for the younger players in our team. Two-legged ties, for instance, are different from sudden-death matches, and my years with Celtic taught me something about the way to approach such matches against the Continentals.

Liverpool's championship success took them into the European Cup, and into European competition for the thirteenth season in succession, and it is not surprising that the players at the Anfield club have learned so much from this regular campaigning against the top teams in Europe.

I know some people were critical of Liverpool during the 1975-76 season – Norwich manager John Bond, for example, who said after Liverpool had won narrowly at Carrow-road that he thought the likes of Manchester United and Queen's Park Rangers would be better for English football, should they win the championship.

The Norwich manager is fully entitled to his opinion, and I would have loved to see Manchester United going on to prove his point; but success is measured in terms of trophies, and the fact remains that at the end of the season, Liverpool had paced themselves so well that they finished up with two items of silverware for the boardroom sideboard, and their players collected a couple of winner's medals apiece.

Ask any professional footballer, and he would tell you that he'd settle for the medals, and never mind the criticisms of the style. That's being down to earth – and Liverpool were realistic enough to know that they should play the way that suited them best. In my book, they emerged as champions worthy of the name, and no one could really deny them the credit their achievements deserved.

In saying this, I am not suggesting that I would rather Manchester United played Liverpool's kind of football. Each team has its own style, and Liverpool have prospered over the years on their own pattern of play. They can be very, very good; and there are times when they put discipline before entertainment. In short, they have got the business of achieving the right results down to a fine art, and any side which can go through sixty or more competitive matches in a season and come up with a trophy or two must be given its due. So you'll not find me grudging in the credit I give to Liverpool for their results – in your heart of hearts, you know as a professional that the winner's medal is the answer to everything and everyone.

Manchester United built their reputation years ago on a somewhat different style of play – a style which put the emphasis on entertainment and attack, on winning games by genuine attacking flair and by carrying the game to the opposition. Liverpool can go forward too, but I think United – on their day – do the job rather better, because we have a certain quality called elegance about us. During the first eighteen months of my career at Old Trafford, I think we were all searching for that formula which provided entertainment, yet also produced the right results. Finally we got it, and settled down to show that it wasn't just a flash in the pan.

So I enjoy playing for Manchester United, as I enjoyed playing for Glasgow Celtic, and the rest of the players at Old Trafford enjoy their football too. Our aim is to put the pressure on the opposition, and while we realise that we risk being caught out at times, we also have the confidence in our own ability which springs from the belief that we can score more goals than we'll concede.

I would never consider playing in Italian club football, because there the defensive attitude dominates, and I know I would feel stifled. I wouldn't like to play in Argentina either – but I could enjoy being a member of the Brazilian international side. Spain wouldn't suit me: not because of the football, but because of the food. Holland or West Germany would be an attractive proposition, because certain teams in those countries have a style of playing which would suit my temperament and compare with my ideas about the way the game should be played. One day, maybe, the Americans will become a force in Soccer, and I could fit into that environment, because I know the States well and I have family connections there.

The United States could be one of the emergent Soccer nations, after many trials and tribulations during the past ten years or so. Now, Soccer does seem to be getting off the ground in America, and youngsters are taking up the game in increasing numbers. There is still a long way to go before the US wins the World Cup, but there is no doubt that the people who are working in Soccer across the Atlantic have this as their ultimate ambition. It would be foolish to dismiss such aspirations as day-dreams, for when the Americans set their minds to something, they usually achieve their objective, and – at the right time – the challenge offered there could be a stimulating experience for someone such as myself.

Undoubtedly the arrival of Pele made an impact, for wherever he played gates went up, and for one exhibition match there was a crowd of more than 58,000. When England played Brazil in the bi-centennial tournament, the attendance at the Los Angeles stadium topped 42,000, despite a sporting counter-attraction. These are all pointers which provide food for thought.

I have ranged a fair way from my starting point, which was Scotland, and I'll close with a few thoughts about Manchester United. We have still got something to learn about maintaining a consistently high level of performance in the First Division of English football, and when you stop to think about it, consistency is what really counts. It's of little value if you go out and play one brilliant game, then give two or three displays which are positively mediocre. Yet such are the demands of an English League season that only teams of the highest calibre can keep on going, right the way through.

You have so many different goals, the day you kick off the season . . . there is the championship, the League Cup, the FA Cup: three competitions, and each of them offering a passport into Europe. Should you qualify for a European competition, that adds to the burden, and it isn't just a matter of playing the matches. You can come up against Derby County on the Saturday, fly 1,000 miles or more for a match against a Continental side the following midweek, fly another 1,000 miles back home, and then have to brace yourselves for a Saturday match against another top-ranking First Division club.

In the old days Manchester United were among the British pioneers in European competition, and our finishing place in the spring of 1976 enabled us to qualify for the UEFA Cup. So the new season added another challenge to the team from Old Trafford. Yet it is impossible for a manager and his players to earmark one particular trophy as the target for the season. These days every game can be like a Cup-tie, because the standard of opposition is so intense.

Some matches may turn out, on the day, to be easier than others; but it remains a fact that there are NO easy games, even against sides which are supposedly inferior. In the First Division, any team is capable of springing a surprise: Norwich City, for instance, who played almost like champions when they went to Anfield and beat Liverpool, and to Elland-road and defeated Leeds.

In the Second Division, and even in the Third or Fourth, there are sides who will raise their game on occasions and score unexpected victories. You have only to think of Colchester beating Leeds in the Cup some years ago, and Crystal Palace winning at Elland-road and at Chelsea in season 1975-76. Remember Southampton and the FA Cup final, too – I certainly do.

Football is an unpredictable game; and Manchester United, on their return to the First Division, proved the truth of this statement . . . even though we became predictable, by achieving one good result after another. Few people expected to see us in contention for the championship and going to Wembley. Manager Tommy Docherty admitted that at the start of the season he believed United would do well enough if they finished around the middle of the table, and that a Cup run would be a bonus.

Yet as the season wore on, he was talking with two voices . . . 'They keep proving me wrong,' he would say about us, as we went from strength to strength; and in the next breath, he was still being cautious: 'I'm not convinced yet that we can go all the way in either competition (the League championship and the FA Cup).'

Well, we confounded The Doc as well as the critics, as Manchester United demonstrated that they could play football of the highest quality, and beat even the best teams in the land. But as we all realise, there is more to it than that.

What I am trying to say here is that United showed they could play football with flair – a great deal of flair – but that we all appreciated we must strive to maintain the standard which marked our return to the First Division . . . and do this, game by game. Season by season, too, I might add. And the only way is to take each game as it comes, just as we did when we were going – however unexpectedly – for the double of the championship and the FA Cup. So there is always a new target at which to aim, no matter how well you may have done, or how much you may have been acclaimed, in the previous season.

I have talked about the possibility of my playing abroad, before my career comes to a close, but I have to admit that I do tend to become attached to clubs. I developed an affection for Glasgow Celtic, even though my ambitions spurred me to travel back south of the Border, after something like seven years at Parkhead; and I have become very attached to Manchester United, and all that the club stands for – a tradition of fine football, a reputation second to none in the world of Soccer, and a future which, I hope and believe, beckons brightly.

That future is one of the reasons why I chose to join Manchester United, in the first place. So now our horizons are the highest honours in football, at home and abroad and, as the title of this book so aptly says, if we remain United, we shall not be moved . . .